CONCEPTUAL DESIGN FOR INTERACTIVE SYSTEMS

Designing for Performance and User Experience

CONCEPTUAL DESIGN FOR INTERACTIVE SYSTEMS

Designing for Performance and User Experience

Avi Parush

AMSTERDAM • BOSTON • HEIDELBERG • LONDON
NEW YORK • OXFORD • PARIS • SAN DIEGO
SAN FRANCISCO • SINGAPORE • SYDNEY • TOKYO

Morgan Kaufmann is an imprint of Elsevier

Acquiring Editor: Todd Green
Editorial Project Manager: Lindsay Lawrence
Project Manager: Punithavathy Govindaradjane
Designer: Matthew Limbert

Morgan Kaufmann is an imprint of Elsevier
225 Wyman Street, Waltham, MA, 02451, USA

Notices
Knowledge and best practice in this field are constantly changing. As new research and experience broaden our understanding, changes in research methods, professional practices, or medical treatment may become necessary.

Practitioners and researchers must always rely on their own experience and knowledge in evaluating and using any information, methods, compounds, or experiments described herein. In using such information or methods they should be mindful of their own safety and the safety of others, including parties for whom they have a professional responsibility.

To the fullest extent of the law, neither the Publisher nor the authors, contributors, or editors, assume any liability for any injury and/or damage to persons or property as a matter of products liability, negligence or otherwise, or from any use or operation of any methods, products, instructions, or ideas contained in the material herein.

ISBN: 978-0-12-419969-9

British Library Cataloguing-in-Publication Data
A catalogue record for this book is available from the British Library

Library of Congress Cataloging-in-Publication Data
A catalogue record for this book is available from the Library of Congress

For information on all MK publications,
visit our website at www.mkp.com

Working together
to grow libraries in
developing countries

www.elsevier.com • www.bookaid.org

Contents

Foreword   ix

Preface   xi
  What Is This Book About?   xi
  Is this book for you?   xiii
  How Is the book organized?   xiv

Acknowledgements   xv

Part 1: The Conceptual Model—Fundamentals   1

Chapter 1: A Multiple and Cross Channel Example: Setting
        an Appointment   3

Chapter 2: Places, Routes, and Abstraction   9

Chapter 3: A Layered Framework for the Conceptual Model   11

Chapter 4: The Function Layer   13
  Functional Chunks   13
  Task-Oriented Chunks   14
  Object-Oriented Chunks   14
  Content-Oriented Chunks   15
  The Relations Between Functional Chunks and Compound Chunks   15

Chapter 5: The Configuration Layer   19
  Conceptual Model Elements   19
  Configuration: The Connections Between the Conceptual Model Elements 20

Chapter 6: The Navigation and Policy Layer   25

The Conceptual Navigation Map: Moving Between Conceptual Model Elements   25
Physical Places for the Conceptual Elements   27
Navigation Policy: The "Rules of the Road"   29
Operational Principles   33

Chapter 7: The Detailed Layers   37

Form: Detailed Conceptual Elements   37
Details: User Interface Elements   39

Chapter 8: Summary of the Components of the Conceptual Model According to the Layered Framework   41

Chapter 9: Conceptual Models Matter!: Implications to Human Performance, Usability, and Experience   43

Usability and User Experience Implications   48

Chapter 10: A Typology of Conceptual Models   51

Sequential and Structured Models   52
Nonsequential and Unstructured Models   55
Is There a Good or a Bad Conceptual Model? Introducing Conceptual Model Complexity   63

Summary of Part 1   67

Part 2: Conceptual Design: A Methodology   69

Chapter 11: Conceptual Design in Context: Think Strategically   71

The Business Context: Motivations for Developing the Product and Value Propositions   71
The Design and Development Context: The User-Oriented Approach   73
Project Management   75

Chapter 12: Conceptual Design: An Overview of the Methodology   77

Revisiting the Framework   77
Project Management Considerations: This Does Not Have to be a Linear Process!   78

Chapter 13: First, User Research. Just Do It   79

Data Collection   79
Analysis   81

Chapter 14: Functional Chunks: Construct the Essential Foundation   89

Define Functional Chunks   90
Link Functional Chunks   93
Checkpoint: Revisit and Revise   97
Project Management Considerations   97

Chapter 15: Configuration: Draw Your First Rough Sketch of the Conceptual Model   99

Define and Configure Conceptual Model Elements   100
Look for a Pivotal Element in the Configuration   100
Reconfigure the Model   103
Checkpoint: Revisit and Revise   104
Project Management Considerations   104

Chapter 16: Navigation Map: Moving from One Place to Another   107

Outline Navigation Map   108
Evaluate and Revise   109
Project Management Considerations   111

Chapter 17: Navigation Policy: Define the "Rules of the Road"   113

Define Physical Places for Conceptual Elements   114
Start Prototyping   118
Define Policy   121
Checkpoint: Revisit and Revise   122
More Implications of the Interaction Channel: The Operational Principles   122
Evaluate and Revise   124
Project Management Considerations   126

Chapter 18: Form: Transition to Detailed Design   129

The Appearance Concept: Consider a Metaphor   130
Add Details   132
Develop a Full Storyboard   133
Test and Revise   134
Project Management Considerations   135

Chapter 19: Summary: Conceptual Design Methodology in a Glance   137

Epilogue: Beyond the conceptual model and onto detailed design   141
References   143
Index   145

Foreword

Technology designers who shape user experiences seek to smooth the path for novices and serve the demanding needs of experts. This was true for fifteenth-century book designers, nineteenth-century train designers, and twenty-first-century smartphone designers. Their innovative designs emerged from a deep empathy for people, sensitivity to diverse social contexts, and imaginative sparks to create new ways of thinking about technology.

When scrolls were reconceived as books, the idea of numbered pages made it possible to have tables of contents, indexes, and cross-references. These breakthrough inventions depended on an understanding of how books would be used differently from scrolls. Similarly, when horse-drawn carriages were reconceived as iron-horse trains and then again as horse-less carriage automobiles, the changes were more profound than giving up on buggy whip holders. New user needs and new technologies required a reconceptualization of the entire user experience. The metaphors, terminology, visual presentation, color, sounds, texture, shapes, and sizes of every component had to be rethought. Then the actions permitted were refashioned to accommodate fresh opportunities and new human needs.

Each generation of designers faces fresh opportunities to remake human experiences in ways that will be easier, safer, more enjoyable, and even more compelling than the past. These considerations were strong in my mind as I developed the direct manipulation concept, which accelerated design thinking by providing a set of principles based on cognitive models. The key principle in the conceptual model was the "visual representation of the objects and actions of interest." For example, the document and file folder icons were the objects and the trash can was a visual representation of the action of deletion. A second direct manipulation principle was "rapid, incremental and reversible operations." The bold change was to shift from keyboard typing of commands to mouse or touchscreen dragging, dropping, clicking, double-clicking, hovering, and other actions directly on the objects and actions of interest.

This direct manipulation formulation of the desktop concept enabled teaching and redesign of many applications. It also triggered the idea of making words selectable as highlighted links that helped make the World Wide Web such a remarkable phenomenon. Direct manipulation also led to varied touchscreen designs including tiny keyboards plus gestures on mobile devices, as well as touchscreen home controls, airport kiosks, and museum exhibits. The direct manipulation conceptual model also triggered interactive information visualization strategies with multiple coordinated windows controlled by dynamic query sliders to filter data items from 5–15 windows simultaneously.

Other conceptual model designers carried old designs into new directions, such as transforming paper books into electronic books and automobile dashboard knobs into touchscreen widgets. However, the greatest success of user experience designers is manifest in the 6 billion users of cell phones. While Moore's Law and other technology advances were important ingredients, I think the designer chefs who cooked up the Web browsers, desktops, and the smartphone apps deserve ample credit for their widely admired contributions. Life has been made better, much of the time, because of the facility for human communication to bind families, e-commerce to promote business, improved healthcare to lengthen and improve quality of life, and much more. Of course, cyber-criminals, scammers, spammers, and terrorists have also taken advantage of these new technologies, reminding us that ease of use and universal access have troubling downsides for which we must remain vigilant.

The remarkable modern Renaissance thinker Buckminster Fuller promoted "comprehensive anticipatory design science" which encouraged designers of new conceptual models to think about future impacts, consider unexpected side effects, respect the needs of diverse stakeholders, and ensure universal usability. He also constantly advanced the awareness of planetary impacts and ethical aspects of design. We should continue to read and be inspired by his thinking.

In summary, the progress of technology brings great opportunities and challenges for designers. There are thousands of books and Web sites about the diverse aspects of design, including design thinking, design methods, design theories, design research, and design science. Novice designers can learn much from these diverse sources, but now Avi Parush provides a fresh perspective on how designers can develop the basic concepts, as well as the attendant information architectures that support clear function, logical configuration, memorable navigation and policy, comprehensible forms, and engaging details. Such layered approaches have been a standard feature of design guides, but Parush walks novice and expert designers through the steps of creating functional chunks, conceptual model elements, physical model elements, detailed conceptual elements, and the user interface elements.

Parush's characterizations are precise and illustrated with helpful examples. His careful choice of wording and clear figures guide readers and clarify the concepts. Of course, every traveler and designer has to find his or her own path, but Parush's valuable guide will help user experience designers to make it even easier for novices to learn new systems, while giving experts even more flexibility.

—**Ben Shneiderman**,
University of Maryland,
February 2015

Preface

WHAT IS THIS BOOK ABOUT?

This book is about conceptual models and conceptual design of interactive systems.

There are so many attractively designed applications. Nevertheless, many leave the user frustrated. What do you need to consider before designing the screens in order to ensure that the application will provide a positive user experience? Conceptual design is a key step in the process of user interface design that answers that question. And this book offers an effective methodology to do conceptual design.

Let us examine a practical example to illustrate where you could encounter conceptual models in the overall context of designing and developing interactive systems. Imagine an application on a mobile device supporting physical workouts. Within such an application, imagine designing the feature of reviewing previous workouts. We can envision a very straightforward 1-2-3 design process consisting of three major steps (Figure 1):

1. Take a few features;
2. Sketch a wireframe, test and revise; and then
3. Finalize the detailed design of the user interface.

However, how exactly did we get from the feature list in step 1 to the detailed wireframe in step 2? There are un-answered questions such as:

- How and when did we decide which items should be grouped? For example, should the "previous workouts" be a group?
- Did we define other *groups* of features? For example, should there be a group of planned workouts?

FIGURE 1:
A hypothetical three-step design process of a mobile application supporting physical workouts.

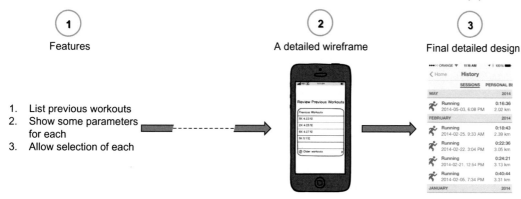

- Did we define the *relations* between the groups? For example, should the planned and previous workout groups be related somehow?
- Did we define if the user should be able to *go* from one group to another? For example, should the user be able to go from the previous workouts group to the planned workouts group?
- Did we determine *where* each of those groups would be? For example, would the previous workouts group be displayed on its own screen or together with planned workouts?
- And more...

These questions and the example reflect a gap in the methodical approach for designing and developing interactive systems. In particular, they reflect a gap between research and requirements (1 in Figure 1), on the one hand, and the detailed design (2 and 3 in Figure 1), on the other hand. However, there is another picture with the gap filled in (2 and 3 in Figure 2).

   This book addresses the critical steps of the *conceptual design* process. The foundation for this process is effective methodology and good science rather than a magic leap involving more art than science. It fills the gap between research and

FIGURE 2:
Conceptual design as the bridge between doing research and determining features, on the one hand, and detailed design, on the other hand.

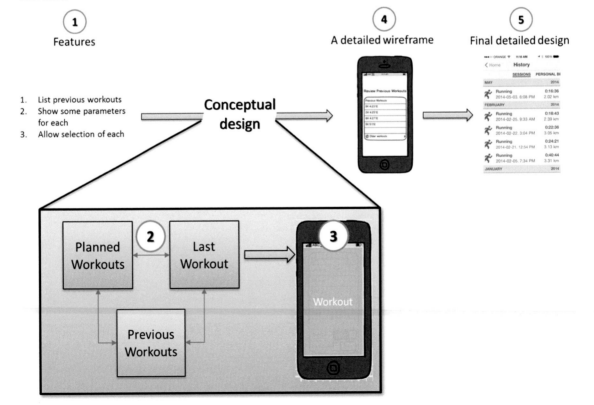

analysis and design. In conceptual design, we define the logical model underlying the interactive system that we design and develop.

Is this book for you?

This book is for you if:

- You design user interfaces.
- You are looking for ways to improve the usability of your product.
- You are looking for a systematic proven foundation to support the creative leap from requirements to design.

If you design user interfaces and are looking for ways to improve the usability of your designs, then this is for you. If you still experience the leap from functional requirements to screen design as a magical mystical experience and you want to introduce a systematic, proven approach, then this is for you. If you review or test user interfaces designed by others and are looking for the words to share your feedback, then this is for you. It is for you whether you are (1) the product manager, (2) the UX or UI designer, (3) the programmer, (4) the marketing person, (5) the graphic designer, (6) an investor, or (7) any other person who has any stake in the product.

Is there any pre-requisite knowledge for using this book? Yes, some. The book focuses on a part of the entire user interface design process: conceptual design. That is why you should know something about the following:

- Fundamentals of user interface, usability, and user experience design
- User-centered or human-oriented design processes
- User research

By studying and using this book, you will achieve two goals:

1. Understand conceptual models in terms of functional chunks, configuration, navigation & policy and in terms of how you can influence human performance, usability, and user experience by the way you define the conceptual model.
2. Implement a solid conceptual design methodology for developing conceptual models.

You can and should devote time to the construction of conceptual models even when you are engaged in an agile or lean development process aimed at expeditiously delivering something to clients and end users. This book challenges the tendency of some developers to think it could be a waste of time to do too much user research, or waste time engaging with wireframes and paper prototypes in exploring various ideas. By engaging in conceptual design instead of skipping this critical phase, you will make the system more usable, saving significant time, money and goods as a result. You can avoid being part of the proliferation of unusable systems and suffer the costs of redesigning those systems to make them effective.

How Is the book organized?

The book has two parts. The first part is a bit theoretical. It focuses on the concept of conceptual models and their impact on human performance, usability, and experience. You can view this part as a primer introducing and discussing this thing we call "a conceptual model." The second part is the practical part. It focuses on the conceptual design process and the methodology with which we develop the conceptual model. The second part walks you through the steps in developing a conceptual model and you can use it as a "how to" guide.

Acknowledgements

This endeavor of writing a book was an enormous undertaking for me. But it was possible because so many have supported and inspired me in the long journey to get here.

First and foremost, Debi, my wife, best friend, and partner. For many years we have worked together in the field of human–computer interaction and you actually understand what this book is all about. We have shared many opportunities to develop and crystallize my views on conceptual design and the methodologies that can help develop conceptual models. Debi, you have enabled my dream to write this book become a reality.

My brother Zeev Parush, who is also an experienced professional in the field of user interface design and user experience. We have discussed and debated design in general, the many challenges in conceptual design, and the significance of engaging in it. Zeev, your valuable comments on an earlier draft of the manuscript helped me rethink and rewrite parts of the book.

Professor Ben Shneiderman has been an inspiration throughout the years. I have learned so much from your pioneering ideas and concepts, and from our discussions on research in human–computer interaction. Your support throughout the various phases of my professional and academic career, and your support and encouragement of this book have been very influential.

Professor Tom Hewett with whom I shared many stimulating and enlightening discussions on a variety of issues in human–computer interaction, research, cognitive psychology, ethics, and the differences between an excellent and mediocre single malt.

Clients with whom I have worked in my years as a practitioner in the field of human–computer interaction. All the projects gave me valuable opportunities to develop my model of user interface design in general and conceptual model, in particular.

Generations of students who had to sit through lectures on an abstract topic such as conceptual design, and yet ask thoughtful questions, challenge my ideas, and push me to keep on refining them.

The reviewers of the original book proposal, my friends and colleagues Professor Ben Shneiderman, Whitney Quesenbery, and Dr Ohad Inbar, who have not only provided very constructive advice for how to write the book, but also encouraged me to write it.

The reviewers of an earlier version of the manuscript, Claire Rowland and Linda Lior, who gave great and constructive feedback that helped me revise the manuscript to become a better book.

The people at Morgan Kaufman, the editors Lindsay Lawrence, Meg Dunkerley, Heather Scherer, the production manager Punitha Govindaradjane, and Todd Green. Your support, patience, and understanding made it all possible.

Finally, my dear parents Miriam and Meir. Growing up in an atmosphere of scholarly writing, my parents encouraged me to pursue my academic interests. As an accomplished author on his own, my father inspired me to write. Thank you for the strong foundation my career is built on.

The Conceptual Model— Fundamentals

So far, the preface and the title of this section suggested that a key concept in this book is the "conceptual model." The objective of the first part of the book is to present the fundamentals of the conceptual model in interactive systems and discuss its impact. Briefly, a conceptual model is the configuration of conceptual elements and the navigation between them. As such, a conceptual model is the foundation of the user interface of any interactive system. However, before we proceed any further with abstract-sounding words and sentences, let us dive into an example. Designing an effective and consistent user experience across the interaction channels is challenging. We will put emphasis in the book on this challenge. The running example for this part of the book is a multiple and cross-channel interaction one.

A Multiple and Cross Channel Example: Setting an Appointment

In order to illustrate the fundamental components of the conceptual model, we introduce and analyze **four existing calendar applications**. Each of the four applications supports setting an appointment and each is on a different interaction channel. Such a comparative illustration can demonstrate how you can achieve the same goal using different conceptual models.

The first step in the interaction flow is common to all four applications: In order to set an appointment, the user can select a starting date and time by pointing at it on the calendar or by activating an option for setting a new appointment. The illustration of the conceptual model starts here after this initial step by looking for what comes next. For the four applications, we will use the following tasks:

1. Defining the basic details of the appointment: topic, place, date, and time.
2. Setting a reminder for the appointment.
3. Setting the appointment as a recurring one.

The sample calendar applications are on the following four interaction channels:

1. Desktop Windows
2. Web-based
3. Tablet
4. Smartphone

The following is a detailed description of the interaction with each of the applications.

The first application for setting an appointment is a well-known Windows-based program typically installed on desktop and laptop computers with a familiar graphical user interface (GUI). In the Calendar user interface, the user can perform these tasks in the very first tab of the Appointment window. The label for that window and the first tab is "Appointment" (Figure 1.1). Notice where and how the user performs each of the following tasks in the GUI:

1. Setting the basic appointment parameters: text fields to specify the subject and location of the appointment, in addition to a couple of controls to specify the date and time of the appointment.
2. Setting a reminder: a pop-down list to select the lead time for the reminder.

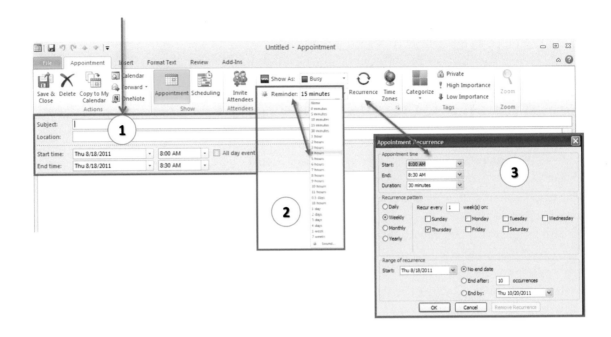

FIGURE 1.1:
A Windows-based GUI application for accomplishing the goal of setting an appointment.

3. Setting a recurrence: includes parameters such as the appointment time, recurrence frequency, and recurrence range of dates.

   The second application is a Web-based calendar. As was the case in the Windows-based application, the interaction flow in this application also allows for starting from a specific time slot in the calendar in which case the date and time are already set based on the starting point (pop-up modal window 1 in Figure 1.2). The user can

1. set up the basic appointment parameters at the top right corner of the page,
2. set a reminder by moving to another place on the page and opening a pop-down list of reminder lead times,
3. set a recurrence by opening of a pop-up modal window, which includes the recurrence frequency and additional parameters.

   The third calendar application is for touch tablets. As with the two previous applications analyzed above, after the interaction starts with the calendar, a dialog box pops up on the screen (1 in Figure 1.3). The user can

1. define immediately and directly at the top of the window the title (purpose) of the appointment and its location;
2. set or edit the date and time of the appointment, a new pop-up modal window appears on top of the previous one, in which the date and time can be set

FIGURE 1.2:
A Web-based application for accomplishing the goal of setting an appointment.

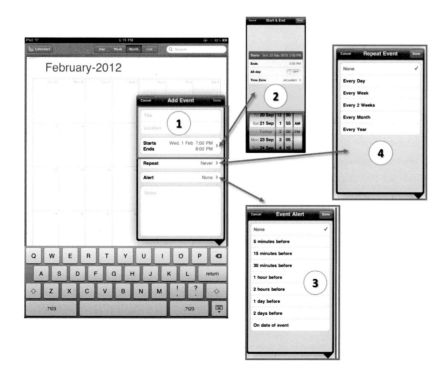

FIGURE 1.3:
A tablet-based application for accomplishing the goal of setting an appointment.

(dismissing the second pop-up and returning to the original main window for setting an appointment conclude this extended interaction);

3. set a reminder opening another pop-up modal window in which the user selects the reminder lead, closes the secondary window, and returns to the main one;

4. set a recurrence of the appointment opening another pop-up modal window in which the user sets the recurrence frequency, closes the secondary window, and returns to the main one.

The fourth application is on a touch-screen smartphone. Creating a new appointment brings the user to a dialog box that fills up the screen (1 in Figure 1.4). The user can

1. define the subject and location of the appointment at the top of the screen, available and visible immediately (the date and time of the appointment are also at the top and available immediately for interaction);

2. set or edit the date of the appointment by opening a small pop-up modal window on top of the appointment screen, but leaving it visible in the background;

3. set the time in a similar way to setting the date (once the parameters are set, the user can conclude this extended interaction by closing the pop-up modal window and returning to the original and main window for setting an appointment);

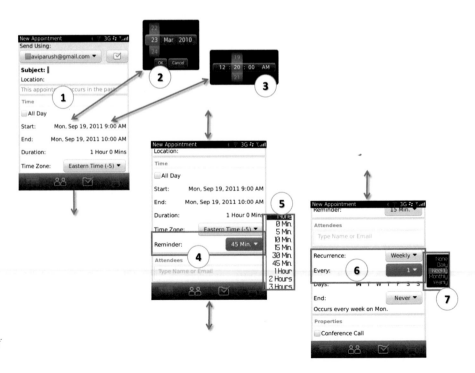

FIGURE 1.4:

A smartphone-based interface for accomplishing the goal of setting an appointment.

4. set a reminder by scrolling down in the same window to the place denoted as 4 in Figure 1.4 (at that place, the user invokes a pop-up list to select the reminder lead times);

5. define the appointment as recurring in which the user scrolls further down to a place denoted as 6 in Figure 1.4 (as before, the user invokes a pop-up lists in order to select the recurrence parameters).

Now that we have four rather simple applications as examples, let us think about them. We know that the four applications support users in achieving the same goals: set an appointment, set a recurring appointment, and set a reminder for the appointment. Yet they look and behave differently. Why? There is an obvious answer: each application runs in a different interaction channel. The design of each application complies with the native look and feel of the respective channel.

However, is that all that is different between them? Moreover, does it matter? Here is the thesis of this book: there are differences that are more fundamental, and yes, they do matter. To elaborate, we shall discuss the conceptual model and show the fundamental differences and their impact. However, before we do that, let us consider one more aspect.

You probably noted that the description of the interaction flow in each of the applications treated each action as if the user "goes" to another "place." Think of "going places" metaphorically. The following sections of this primer discuss the relation between "places" and elements of the conceptual model and their relation to "physical places" such as windows, dialog boxes, and Web pages. We call this the spatial metaphor. Next, we discuss the significance of spatial metaphor and the importance of abstraction when dealing with the conceptual model.

Places, Routes, and Abstraction

A very common term when designing a website is information architecture. The use of the term "architecture" implies talking about the basic function, configuration, and layout. Just look at any architectural plan, such as the one in Figure 2.1.

The plan is rather minimalist with respect to providing any details. All it provides is the general layout of spaces serving a given function (e.g., kitchen and bedroom), the location of each such place in the overall configuration relative to other places. In addition, by depicting doors and passages, it gives us clear information regarding the routes one should take to navigate from one place to another. Yet, as minimalist as it is, the drawing is highly useful in assessing the architectural plan before proceeding to implement it: Are all desired functions provided for (e.g., that there is a place for the den)? Is there enough space allocated for each function (e.g., dining and living room should be the largest place)? Is access to rooms appropriate? Do the routes and distances between places support easy navigation from one place to another? In other words, a typical architectural plan provides us with the global features first before introducing the details.

The representation of the conceptual models is similar to the architectural plan. It helps to ensure that there is a "place" for each function and that the routes for navigating from one place to another support the interaction workflow adequately. How can we best visually represent such global features before getting into the details? To analyze and discuss conceptual models, we use the visual language of boxes and arrows. In other words, we are talking about conceptual models in rather abstract terms that are void of any details. Why is it important to remain on the abstract level when designing and discussing the conceptual model before getting into the details?

The abstract representation of the conceptual models supports well one of the fundamental characteristics of human perception and understanding. A classic research on human perception and attention (Navon, 1977) suggests that the global structure of a visual scene tends to precede perception of any local features, rather than perceiving all features at once. The original study used stimuli similar to those in Figure 2.2. The findings of the study suggest that people respond faster to perceiving the letter "H" in both the left and the right elements in Figure 2.2, compared to identifying from which characters the large "H" is composed of ("H" in the left-hand stimulus and "S" in the right-hand stimulus). The large letter "H" is considered as a global feature of the

FIGURE 2.1:
A simple architectural plan.

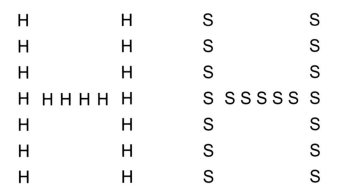

FIGURE 2.2:
Stimuli used in the Navon (1977) original study of global precedence.

visual scene, and the letters composing the large letter are considered as local features or the details. This is referred to as "global precedence." In general, the global precedence hypothesis claims that the processing of a visual scene begins with attention to the global properties first followed by local as time progresses.

We can consider the abstract representation of the conceptual model as representing the global features of the model, and later on, when we add all the details, those will be the local features. Such representation of the conceptual model is sufficient for an early assessment of the implications for human performance and user experience. Stakeholders assess the conceptual model better when we first encounter the "global features" of the model before immersing ourselves in the details. Consistent with the natural "global precedence" in our visual perception and understanding is our use of the spatial metaphor and spatial terms when we talk about conceptual models.

A Layered Framework for the Conceptual Model

We are going to use a layered framework to define and analyze the conceptual model. Why layered? Think of the layered onion metaphor. The idea behind this popular metaphor is that we peel off one layer after another to reach the core and discover the real taste of the onion. When it comes to user interfaces of interactive systems, we can take what we see in the UI as the outer layer and imagine there are inner and hidden layers that we need to peel off to uncover the core.

In the first part of the book where we introduce and analyze conceptual models, we peel off layers to uncover the core, the underlying conceptual model. In the second part of the book where we methodically construct a conceptual model, we go the other way: we add one layer on top of another, from the abstract to the most concrete. Figure 3.1 shows the layered framework representing the entire context in which the conceptual model resides.

The framework, from the bottom up, consists of five layers:

1. The *function* level consists of functional chunks—*groups of tasks and objects and their associated parameters* that the user uses to accomplish goals.
2. The *configuration* level consists of the conceptual model elements—*the metaphorical "places"* the user must visit to perform each set of functions and the links between the "places."
3. The *navigation and policy* level depicts the navigation and navigation rules—*the "routes" the user takes between "places,"* the physical elements containing one or more conceptual "places," and the policy governing the interrelations among the physical elements.
4. The *form* level consists of *detailed conceptual elements* serving as the transition from conceptual to detailed design.
5. The *details* level consists of user interface elements—*detailed look and feel* of each UI element at each place the user visits to perform tasks.

The conceptual design deals with **what** the user does and **where**, but without the details. In terms of this framework, conceptual design spans the function, configuration, and navigation and policy levels. The transition to the detailed design takes place on the form level, introducing details and finally transforming the conceptual design into a full and detailed user interface.

FIGURE 3.1:
The layered framework representing the conceptual model and detailed design.

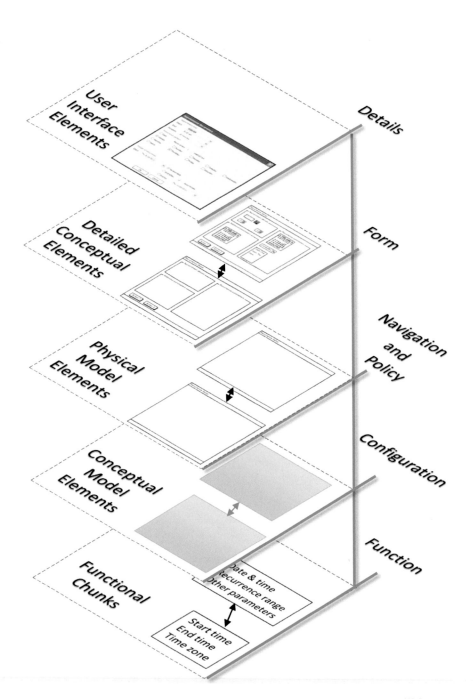

Throughout the analysis and discussion of the conceptual model, we will be peeling the onion layers. In other words, we will reverse engineer the calendar examples from the previous chapter to uncover the elements and characteristics of their respective underlying conceptual models.

The Function Layer

FUNCTIONAL CHUNKS

Many drivers determine the functions of the product: needs of users and any other stakeholder, product vision and definition, business objectives and model, and technology. The outcome is what we have on the function layer. It includes all the parameters, information items, and actions that are relevant to the domain of the application or system (e.g., time management). Combined, all of these represent the functionality of the product.

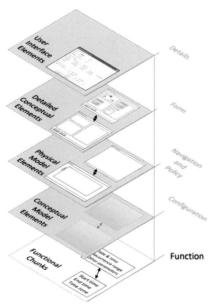

Designers typically group parameters, information items, and actions pertaining to a given domain into functional chunks according to a common purpose or meaning for the user. They define functional chunks based on the relevant research and analysis (user, market, etc.). The functional chunks can revolve around tasks and/or objects. In this book, we focus on the two primary forms of functional chunks: task-oriented and object-oriented. There is another form of functional chunk and that is the content-oriented chunk. We will mention it here but the methodology part of the book will not focus on it. Defining these functional chunks is a part of the conceptual design process. The second part of the book deals with the methodology of conceptual design.

TASK-ORIENTED CHUNKS

Task-oriented functional chunks are collections of tasks serving a common purpose (see Figure 4.1). Task-oriented chunks enable the user to reach a tangible goal, accomplish something concrete (such as set an appointment or set a reminder or get information about a specific topic). A task-oriented chunk could also be purely for fun and engagement with no tangible utility (e.g., a game task such as "place all the cards in order according to a set of rules").

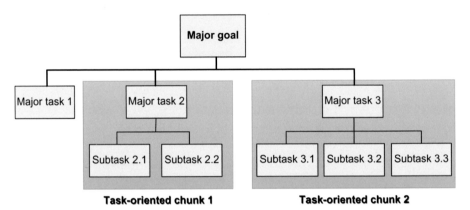

FIGURE 4.1:
The idea of a task-oriented chunk.

OBJECT-ORIENTED CHUNKS

Object-oriented chunks include an object from the subject matter of the application domain (e.g., an appointment, a printer, a page, a trip, or a parking location) with tasks relevant to that object (Figure 4.2) (Shneiderman, 1998).

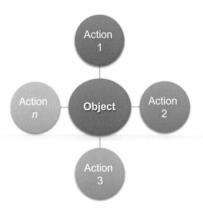

FIGURE 4.2:
The idea of an object-oriented chunk.

CONTENT-ORIENTED CHUNKS

Content-oriented chunks are collections of information items. Each chunk is a content category. Users typically search for and use the information items for various purposes (Figure 4.3).

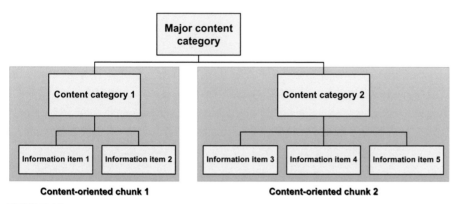

FIGURE 4.3:
The idea of a content-oriented chunk.

THE RELATIONS BETWEEN FUNCTIONAL CHUNKS AND COMPOUND CHUNKS

Often, a single functional chunk does not fully support the completion of a task. More often, it does not support the accomplishment of user goals. In such cases, we look for several interrelated chunks to support task completion and/or goal achievement. We can even have several task, object, and content chunks making up a compound chunk (Figure 4.4). Having several chunks within a compound chunk depends on how strong the relations between the chunks are. The strength of the relations depends on frequency of use, task structure, and interaction flow. Let us look at a small example to clarify. In order to support users in preparing to print something, we can have a compound functional chunk including objects such as the printer and the page, and these are related to task-oriented chunk including opening, changing, removing, saving, and printing.

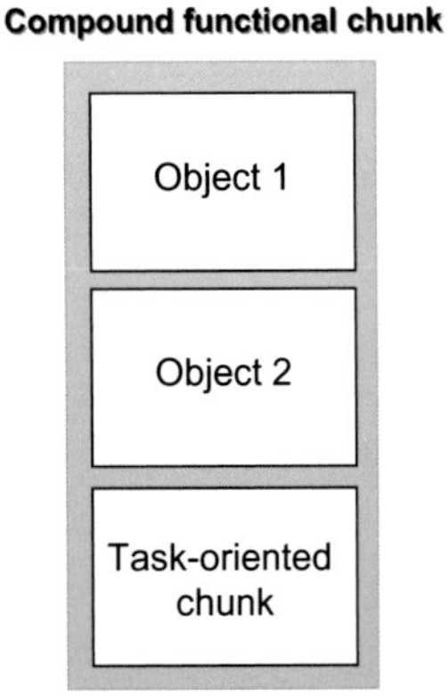

FIGURE 4.4:
*The idea of a compound
functional chunk.*

Compound functional chunk

Functional chunks in the appointment example

The four applications implemented on different channels serve the same function: setting the various parameters of a new appointment. This common function seems to bond, in each of the applications, three chunks of parameters and actions aimed at supporting the accomplishment of that function. The "functional chunks" in the example of the appointment setup applications include the following:

- Subgoal 1: Define the details of the appointment.
  - The parameters: Title of the meeting, the date and time, and finally the location of the meeting.
  - The actions: Approve or cancel the definition of the appointment details.
- Subgoal 2: Set a reminder.
  - The parameters: Time before the start of the appointment.
  - The actions: Approve or cancel the parameters.
- Subgoal 3: Define a recurrence for the appointment.
  - The parameters: Recurrence in terms of frequency or number of times within a given period.

The contents of the functional chunks reflect what the user does. A hierarchical task structure can represent this formally. The root of the task tree is the main goal of the user: define the key details of the appointment, common to all four applications. This goal is further broken down into three subgoals and their associated actions (Figures 4.4 and 4.5).

Are the functional chunks in this example task-oriented or object-oriented? It seems that all parameters and actions revolve around an abstract object: an appointment. Thus, all parameters and actions related to setting an appointment can be viewed as a single object-oriented functional chunk. However, there is a separate functional chunk for

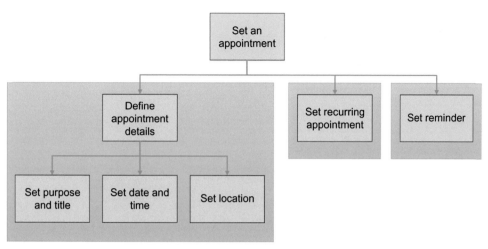

FIGURE 4.5:
The task structure for accomplishing the goal of setting an appointment with a focus on the three functional chunks for each of the subgoals.

each of the subgoals and those are task-oriented functional chunks. In the methodology part of the book, we will discuss the construction of functional chunks, but for now, this example can already be an indicator that often, functional chunks of a different nature, task- or object-oriented, are combined to serve better the high-level user goal.

The Configuration Layer

The configuration layer is the abstraction of the functional chunks along with their relations. The result is conceptual model elements configured according to the relations between them. In other words, we can refer to this as the functional architecture.[1]

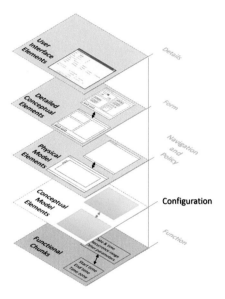

CONCEPTUAL MODEL ELEMENTS

User interaction typically involves doing something, then often "transitioning" to do something else, and so on until accomplishing the goal. As discussed earlier, we tend to use a spatial metaphor to describe such an interaction flow. The spatial metaphor talks about "places" the user visits and navigates among them. Thus, the underpinnings of user interaction with the functional chunks are the different "places" the user visits in order to perform tasks and accomplish goals. These "places" are the most fundamental elements of the conceptual model. Relations between functional chunks translate to

---

[1]Equivalent to information architecture in the world of Web site design, but in conceptual design of interactive systems, information is but one category of elements in the architecture, in addition to tasks, objects, and their parameters.

connections between "places," and **the entire configuration of interconnected "places" supports user goals**.

Designed properly, these elements have two fundamental characteristics:

1. Support, fully or partially, performing at least one *task* (e.g., set an appointment or set a reminder).
2. Provide the user with an ***interaction*** opportunity for performing the task and accomplishing the goal. Thus, the conceptual element is an interactive element.

CONFIGURATION: THE CONNECTIONS BETWEEN THE CONCEPTUAL MODEL ELEMENTS

The configuration of interconnected "places" can support the completion of tasks, particularly tasks involving many actions and parameters. The strength of the connection between conceptual elements is an additional characteristic of the relations between them. Some connections are stronger due to frequency of interaction or that one task depends upon another or tasks that are functionally similar. Following that, there could be various ways to configure connected elements to support different tasks and interaction flows with varying connection strengths.

In order to model the "places," whereby each "place" is the container of a functional chunk, and the connections between them, we represent each "place" as an empty box. Lines linking the boxes represent the connections between the conceptual model elements. The schematic graphical representation of the underlying configuration as boxes and lines is your very first "napkin sketch." Some may refer to it as the most basic wireframe.[2] Using such visual representations, Figure 5.1 illustrates how different configurations of four conceptual elements can result in three different conceptual models.

Figure 5.1 shows the elements linked in a sequence in configuration A. In such a configuration, two of the elements (1 and 4) are linked to just another element, and two of the elements (2 and 3) are each linked to two other elements. In configuration B, each of the elements is linked with two other elements. In addition, each element lacks a link to one other element in the structure. Finally, in configuration C, two elements (1 and 2) have each a link to two other elements, and the two remaining elements (3 and 4) have each a link to a single element. These different configurations represent different models and have direct implications for

---

[2]Wireframes themselves can appear and be utilized on several abstraction levels, that is, with varying degrees of details. This will be discussed further later in the primer part of the book and the second part of the book outlining the methodology for constructing a conceptual model.

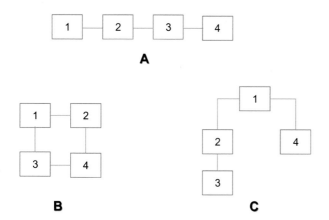

FIGURE 5.1:
*Three possible
configurations of four
conceptual model
elements, representing
three different conceptual
models.*

reaching from one element to another as will be discussed soon with respect to the conceptual navigation map.

Conceptual models in the appointment example

Here is how we peel the onion layers to get to the core. To uncover the configuration underlying each of the appointment setup applications, we blur out the details from the screens and windows and define an abstract "place" for the functional chunk. This results in a conceptual model element. Figure 5.2 shows how we peel off a couple of layers to reach the concept underlying the UI.

The outer concrete layer has all the details of the UI. When we blur out the details of the UI, we have a blank representation of the UI components in the middle inner layer, two windows in the example. As we peel away more details, we reach the deepest layer, the core. This layer shows each window as a box, arrows showing the route, and numbers indicating the order of interaction with the windows in performing the task.

> To uncover the underlying conceptual model, look for the following:
>
> • The "places" where the user interacts with the application to accomplish tasks and goals.
>
> • The "routes" the user takes in order to get from one "place" to another.

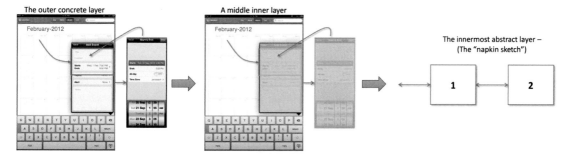

FIGURE 5.2:
Three layers representing the UI and its underlying conceptual model.

Table 5.1 shows the uncovering of the fundamental conceptual model underlying each of the four calendar applications.

TABLE 5.1:

A comparison of the conceptual models across the four applications for setting an appointment

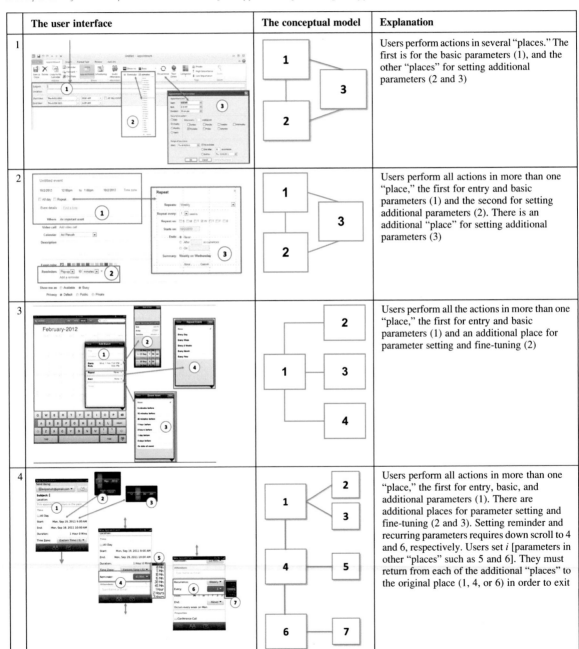

	The user interface	The conceptual model	Explanation
1			Users perform actions in several "places." The first is for the basic parameters (1), and the other "places" for setting additional parameters (2 and 3)
2			Users perform all actions in more than one "place," the first for entry and basic parameters (1) and the second for setting additional parameters (2). There is an additional "place" for setting additional parameters (3)
3			Users perform all the actions in more than one "place," the first for entry and basic parameters (1) and an additional place for parameter setting and fine-tuning (2)
4			Users perform all actions in more than one "place," the first for entry, basic, and additional parameters (1). There are additional places for parameter setting and fine-tuning (2 and 3). Setting reminder and recurring parameters requires down scroll to 4 and 6, respectively. Users set i [parameters in other "places" such as 5 and 6]. They must return from each of the additional "places" to the original place (1, 4, or 6) in order to exit

The configuration of the conceptual elements reflects the "places" users visit and the links between the "places" enabling the performance of tasks and accomplishment of goals. Comparing the four conceptual models in Table 5.1 indicates that each, while serving a similar function, is very different with respect to the number of conceptual elements and their configuration, particularly applications 3 and 4 being very different from each other and from 1 and 2.

The configuration of the conceptual elements by itself does not fully reflect the strength of the links between the elements. In addition, it does not provide the details of the navigation through the configuration. We still need the navigation map, the assignment of the conceptual elements to physical places, and the navigation policy. These are on the next layer in the conceptual design framework.

The Navigation and Policy Layer

The spatial metaphor continues to serve us well in describing the conceptual model of interactive systems. We use the term "navigation" to describe users getting from one place to another. We use the term "navigation map" to represent the route instructions, as it were, throughout the conceptual model. Here are some details about navigation and navigation maps.

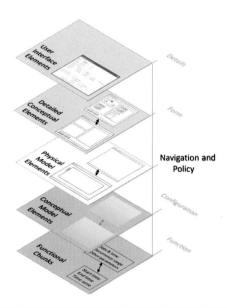

THE CONCEPTUAL NAVIGATION MAP: MOVING BETWEEN CONCEPTUAL MODEL ELEMENTS

The conceptual navigation map shows "routes" the user can or is required to take through the configuration to perform and conclude all required steps for accomplishing a goal. Showing "routes" in the navigation map includes the following:

1. The entry and exit points for starting and concluding the interaction.
2. The direction of each link between conceptual elements in the configuration; some links are one-way and some are two-way.

Figure 6.1 shows one conceptual model configuration (configuration C from Figure 5.1) with three different navigation maps.

In conceptual navigation map C1, navigation starts and ends with conceptual model element 1. From that element, one can proceed to conceptual model element 2 or 4. When one concludes the interaction at conceptual model element 2 or 4, one navigates back to conceptual model element 1 in order to exit. Finally, one can continue from conceptual model element 2 to conceptual model element 3, and once one concludes the interaction in conceptual model element 3, one has to navigate back to conceptual model element 2. Conceptual navigation map C2 is identical to C1 with the exception that one can conclude the interaction in conceptual model element 4 and exit from there without having to go back to conceptual model element 1. Finally, in conceptual navigation map C3, one can also conclude the interaction in conceptual model elements 2 and 3 and exit from each of them without having to retrace the navigation backward in order to exit.

The following two primary considerations influence the route a user takes between linked conceptual model elements to perform all the tasks required to accomplish a goal:

1.   The conceptual model configuration
2.   Decisions on the workflow and dynamics of the interaction

Each of the links in a conceptual model configuration is a possible route the user can take. However, having a link between elements does not always tell us if it is a one-way or a two-way route. In addition, it does not tell us where the entry and exit points are. The decision on those latter parameters is influenced by workflow.

However, the physical location of each conceptual element also influences the route characteristics. For example, look at elements 2 and 3 in any of the three examples in Figure 6.1. The map indicates that there is a two-way route between these two elements. Will the navigation be the same if each of the two elements is in a separate window as compared to a case where both elements are in the same window but are in two separate tabs? This brings us to the next important aspect of the conceptual model: physical

FIGURE 6.1:
Three possible navigation maps for the same configuration of conceptual elements.

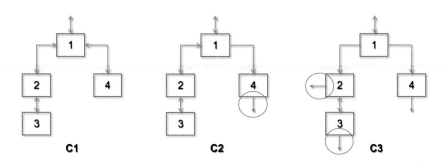

places. In particular, we will discuss how the physical place of conceptual elements can affect navigation and interaction.

PHYSICAL PLACES FOR THE CONCEPTUAL ELEMENTS

So far, we used the spatial term "places" to talk about conceptual elements. It is very important to emphasize that this is in a strict metaphorical sense and not in the physical sense of places. However, the correspondence between the metaphorical "places" and their physical location is significant when we determine that physical location, the "distances" between "places," and the navigation among them.

Conceptual model elements could sometimes have a correspondence of one-to-one with their physical location. For example, a "place" could be a window. Yet, at other times, there would not be such correspondence. For example, Figure 6.2 illustrates

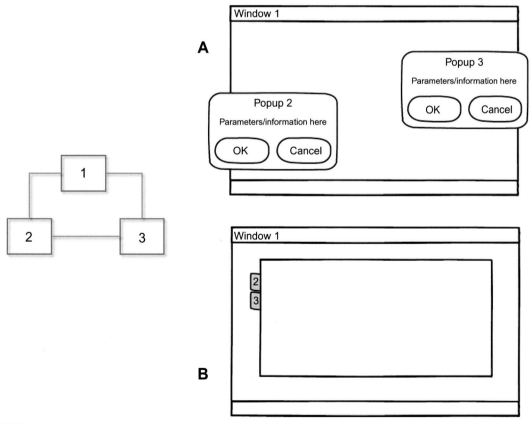

FIGURE 6.2:
Different physical assignments for a conceptual model with three elements.

a configuration of three conceptual elements representing three metaphorical "places" with "place" 1 linked to "places" 2 and 3. These metaphorical "places" can be located physically in various ways.

The three elements could be in three distinct physical places (e.g., three windows as in A in Figure 6.2). Such a model would reflect link strength that is similar between element 1 and elements 2 and 3, respectively. It could also reflect two similar (same frequency or same importance) interaction flows, from element 1 to element 2 or from element 1 to element 3.

Alternatively, "places" 2 and 3 can be located within a single physical place hosting also conceptual element 1 (see B in Figure 6.2). Such a configuration would represent tighter relations between element 1 as a parent to elements 2 and 3. It could also reflect an interaction flow between elements 2 and 3 that must remain within the context of the parent element 1.

Figure 6.3 illustrates another scheme for assigning conceptual elements to physical places. Element 1 is linked to elements 2 and 4 in the conceptual model. In addition, element 3 is linked with element 4. One possible physical assignment for this model is shown in A; "places" 2 and 3 can physically appear within a single physical place

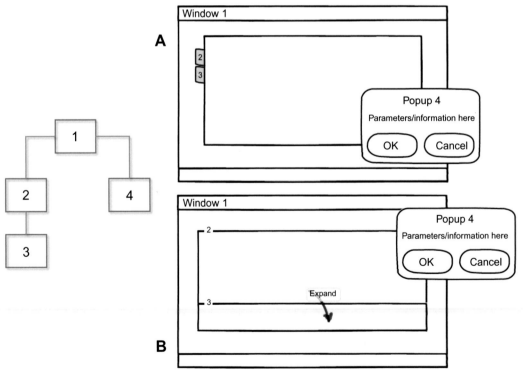

FIGURE 6.3:
Different physical assignments for a conceptual model with four elements.

hosting also conceptual element 1, whereas "place" 4 appears as a pop-up window. This assignment reflects the tighter link between elements 2 and 3 and their "distance" from element 4. Alternatively, a possible hierarchical link between elements 2 and 3 can be physically assigned such that elements 2 and 3 appear as "places" within the window hosting also conceptual element 1, with element 3 being an expansion of element 2. Element 4 is assigned to a separate pop-up window.

Determining the assignment of the conceptual elements to physical places has significant implications on the navigation map and navigation policy. As is discussed soon in this part of the book, it also has implications to human performance, usability, and user experience.

NAVIGATION POLICY: THE "RULES OF THE ROAD"

Effective map and route instructions must include the rules that govern the navigation. Can we go anywhere we want at any time we want? Similarly, the conceptual navigation map must include those rules, which we refer to as the navigation policy.

Design decisions regarding the conceptual navigation map go hand in hand with decisions regarding the physical places and the policy of the navigation. These decisions must consider a fundamental question: Should the user be able to perform more than one task at a time? In terms of interaction flow, the implications of this question are the following: Is the user required to fully or partially complete a task before moving on to the next task, and is the user required to complete a given task, move on to another task and complete it, and then return to complete the original task?

In terms of the conceptual model, the policy deals fundamentally with the challenge of *modality*: While interacting with a given conceptual element in a given physical place, can the user also interact with another conceptual element, in the same physical place or different places? When the answer to this question is yes, we refer to it as a modeless policy. A modeless conceptual model element allows interactions with other conceptual model elements at the same time. When the policy confines the user to interacting with only one conceptual element in a single physical place at a time, we refer to it is a modal policy. A modal conceptual model element is one that does not allow interaction with any other conceptual model element at the same time.

The conceptual navigation map in Figure 6.4 is an example of the relations between the navigation policy and the physical places of the conceptual elements. The navigation policy shown in part A of Figure 6.4 allows the user to interact simultaneously with conceptual model element 2 in "place" 2 and with element 3 in "place" 3. The physical assignment is such that the user can then close conceptual model element 3, conclude the task with conceptual model element 2, and go back to conceptual model element 1, which is in "place" 1. The navigation policy shown in part

FIGURE 6.4:
*Conceptual navigation
map with two physical
assignments reflecting
different navigation
policies.*

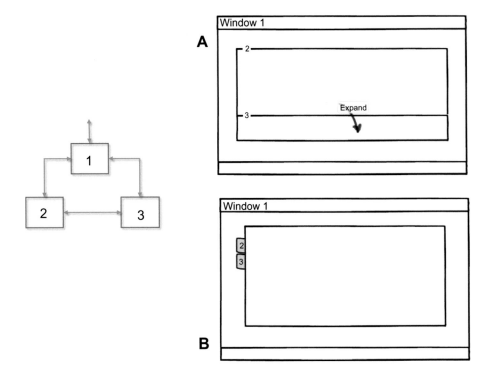

B of Figure 6.4 allows the user to interact only with conceptual model element 2, with the option to proceed to conceptual model element 3, complete the task there, then return to conceptual model element 2, complete the task there, and then go back to conceptual model element 1.

The examples in Figure 6.4 tell us something about the concept of modality in interactive systems. Dealing with modality and making decisions regarding its scope are critical to finalizing the navigation map and policy. Table 6.1 shows a simple categorization of the relations between physical place assignment of conceptual elements and modality.

The categorization has two possibilities for physical place assignment of conceptual elements: the elements are located in the same physical place or located in different physical places.

There are also two possibilities for modality: interaction with the conceptual elements is independent, that is, the user can interact with more than one element simultaneously, or mutually exclusive, that is, the user can interact with only one conceptual element at a time.

Note that the interaction channel also plays a role when it comes to considering physical place assignment and modality. Table 6.1 shows different examples for

TABLE 6.1:

Examples of physical place assignment of two conceptual elements, in the same or different places, and modality

		Physical place assignment	
		Same place	**Different place**
Modality	Modeless: independent	Window Name — Group 1 / Group 2	Window 1 / Window 2
	Modal: mutually exclusive in a large-screen channel	Window 1 (tabs 2, 3)	Window Name / Dialogue Name — OK / Cancel

Continued

TABLE 6.1:
Examples of physical place assignment of two conceptual elements, in the same or different places, and modality—cont'd

	Physical place assignment	
	Same place	**Different place**
Modal: mutually exclusive in a small-screen channel		

mutually exclusive modality in a large-screen channel (e.g., desktop) in comparison with a small-screen channel (e.g., a mobile phone).

OPERATIONAL PRINCIPLES

We have already mentioned, more than once, that characteristics of the interaction channel such as screen size and native look and feel are some of the essential criteria for making decisions throughout the conceptual design process. Following this, an additional important characteristic of interaction channels is the physical way the user interacts through the channel. The simplest examples for physically interacting with a desktop computer are the keyboard and mouse. The keyboard lets the user enter text, issue commands, navigate, invoke programs, and control devices (e.g., disk drive, sound volume, and lighting). The mouse lets the user achieve direct manipulation of on-screen elements through operations such as point-and-click and drag-and-drop (Shneiderman, 1982, 1983). As we move on to touch-based channels, physical gestures, such as single touch, long touch, swipe, multifinger touch, multifinger gestures, and more, let the user perform various operations such as selecting and moving and zooming and more. In addition, there are channels based on other modalities and senses such as speech, gaze, brain activity, and gross gestures in a virtual space. The operational principles describe the channel's characteristics of the physical interaction and should be part of the conceptual design (Shneiderman & Plaisant, 2010).

The operational principles can influence the navigation map and policy and the assignment of conceptual elements to physical places. Let us examine a few examples illustrating the implications of the operational principles on the design decisions, presented in Table 6.2. All examples are based on the same conceptual model presented at the top row of the table. When we examine the two alternative sets of operational principles in a desktop computer, we see that those can have some influence on the conceptual design. Using a mouse without an embedded wheel, the user can navigate between elements 1 and 2 by pointing and clicking. Assigning the two elements to two tabs, one next to the other, minimizes travel to the place where the user can initiate this navigation. In addition, using an embedded wheel, the user can navigate between the two elements by wheel-based scrolling so the designer can assign the two elements to the same physical place. This also gives the advantage of more than one element visible at a time. When we examine the operational principles in the mobile device, one option is a device that includes a stylus-based point and touch operation. In this case, the designer assigned each of the two conceptual elements to a different physical place with an option to navigate between them with the touch of the stylus. In the other option, we have a device providing a touch-based gesture interaction (such as swiping). In this case, the designer

TABLE 6.2:
Examples of operational principles and their associated conceptual design in desktop and mobile interaction channels

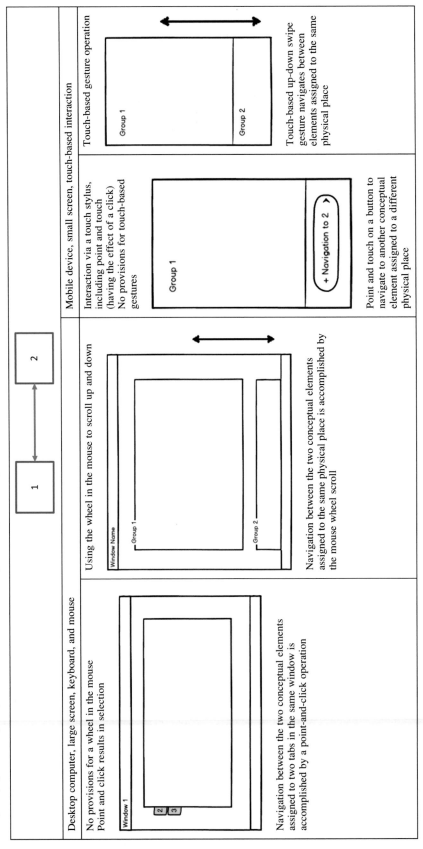

	1	2
	Desktop computer, large screen, keyboard, and mouse	**Mobile device, small screen, touch-based interaction**
	Using the wheel in the mouse to scroll up and down	Touch-based gesture operation
	No provisions for a wheel in the mouse Point and click results in selection	Interaction via a touch stylus, including point and touch (having the effect of a click) No provisions for touch-based gestures
	Navigation between the two conceptual elements assigned to two tabs in the same window is accomplished by a point-and-click operation	Navigation between the two conceptual elements assigned to the same physical place is accomplished by the mouse wheel scroll	Point and touch on a button to navigate to another conceptual element assigned to a different physical place	Touch-based up-down swipe gesture navigates between elements assigned to the same physical place

assigned both conceptual elements to the same physical place and the user navigates between via an up-down touch-based swiping gesture.

Navigation maps and policies in the appointment case study

In this section, we take another comparative look at the four example applications of setting an appointment. The conceptual models are presented here (Table 6.3) in terms of both the conceptual elements and their physical places, along with the navigation map and the navigation policy.

The four examples illustrate what happens to the configuration of the conceptual elements once they are assigned to physical places and how this assignment influences the navigation map and policy.

TABLE 6.3:

A comparison of the conceptual models, their places along with the navigation maps and policies, across the four applications for setting an appointment

The user interface	The conceptual model	The conceptual model + navigation map and policy
1 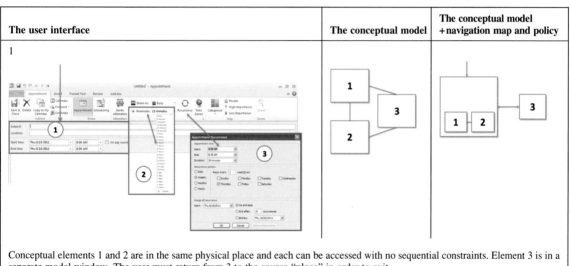		
Conceptual elements 1 and 2 are in the same physical place and each can be accessed with no sequential constraints. Element 3 is in a separate modal window. The user must return from 3 to the source "place" in order to exit		
2 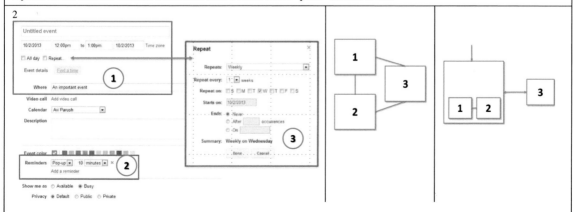		
Conceptual elements 1 and 2 are in the same physical place and each can be accessed with no sequential constraints. Element 3 is in a separate modal window. The user must return from 3 to the source "place" in order to exit		

Continued

TABLE 6.3:
A comparison of the conceptual models, their places along with the navigation maps and policies, across the four applications for setting an appointment—cont'd

The user interface	The conceptual model	The conceptual model +navigation map and policy
3 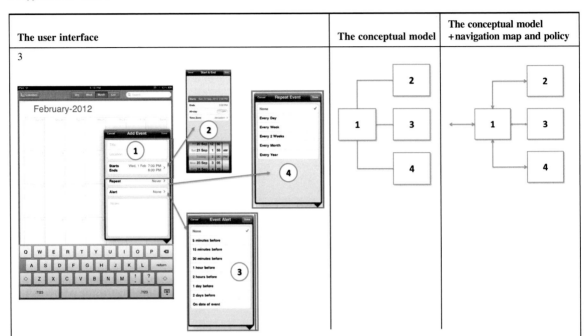		
All conceptual elements are in separate physical places, all modal windows. The user must return from each of the additional places, 2, 3, and 4, to the original place (1) in order to exit		
4 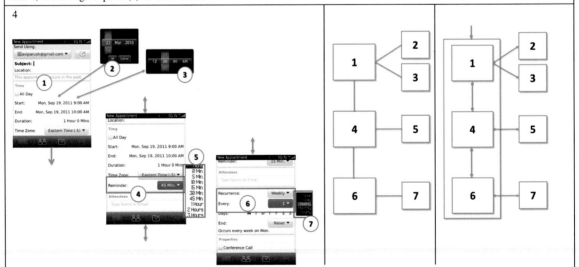		
Conceptual elements 1, 4, and 6 are all in the same physical place. The user can access them with no sequential constraints. Due to the small screen size, elements 1, 4, and 6 may require scrolling to access them. There are additional places for parameter setting and fine-tuning (2 and 3). Places 2, 3, 5, and 7 are modal and require a return trip to the source place		

The Detailed Layers

The analysis so far dealt with the conceptual model at a relatively high abstraction level. That is, the elements in the model are void of any details. Now, we have reached the layers where we see more details in the concept. This is a transitional layer where decisions influence the conceptual model and consequently performance and usability, on the one hand, and introduce details into the design, on the other hand.

FORM: DETAILED CONCEPTUAL ELEMENTS

In the form layer, the conceptual elements have some details from each of the chunks (information, parameters, and actions) in consideration of the physical assignment and the navigation map and policy. Detailed conceptual design involves preliminary decisions about the controls and preliminary visual design considerations (for a visual user interface).

There could be *several granularity levels* for the transitional phase between conceptual to detailed conceptual elements. These depend on the definition of the functional chunks

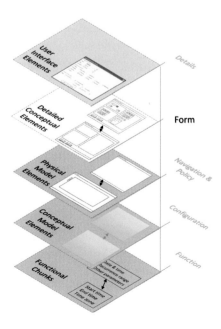

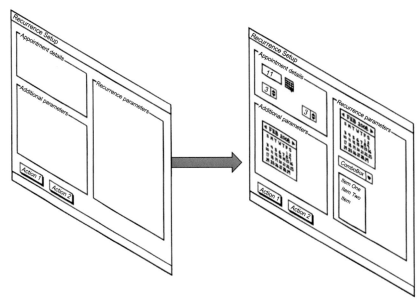

FIGURE 7.1:
Two granularity levels of conceptual model elements in the form layer.

and the needs for their representation. Figure 7.1 shows two granularity levels for a given conceptual model element in the form layer. The left-hand element shows the design decision that the conceptual model element contains a functional chunk composed of several subchunks, all of them assigned to the same physical place. Note that this granularity level still lacks much detail, thus allowing the design and evaluation of the fundamental structure of the conceptual model with no "distractions." The right-hand element has the parameters and controls the user interacts with and a more detailed visual layout. You can use this level of granularity for user testing.

Decisions about controls are typically a two-step process. One is fine-tuning the decisions about the physical places hosting the conceptual elements and the navigation policy. For example, the designer can assign several conceptual elements to the same physical place such as a window or a web page. Such elements would be those that the user needs to see or act upon together, or interaction with one element following the other. However, the designer can fine-tune the decision to place the conceptual elements in separate areas on the window or under separate tabs or selected through a menu. Such decisions span the transition between conceptual and detailed design, because on the one hand, they reflect the nature and relations between functional chunks and impact navigation map and policy, and on the other hand, they involve decisions about specific controls. This brings us into the details in the UI. On top of that, the transition phase between conceptual and detailed design can include decisions about specific controls that have negligent impact on the conceptual model. Such decisions may include, for example, whether setting of a numerical parameter will be done by entering a number into a text field or selected from a predefined list or via a spinner-type control (see examples in the right-hand sketch in Figure 7.1).

Finally, determining initial visual design is also part of the transition from conceptual to detailed design. Overall, visual layout reflects the functional chunks and their interrelations and can thus affect the conceptual model and its implications (e.g., impact on visual search). Another aspect of the visual design is a choice of a metaphor. As examples, the desktop and the hand calculator are enduring visual metaphors for many operating systems and applications. A choice of an appropriate metaphor is highly relevant to users' mental models. The metaphor could fit existing mental models (e.g., a visual metaphor of a pocket calendar could be appropriate for a calendar application) or could support users in constructing a new mental model that can in turn facilitate a better understanding of an application.

DETAILS: USER INTERFACE ELEMENTS

As the design process unfolds, we reach the top layer in the conceptual and detailed design framework: the details layer. We add more details to the elements making up the user interface. Such details include finalized decisions about controls, visual layout (e.g., exact locations of controls and information items), graphic design (e.g., colors, fonts, and icons), terminology, and any other open issues regarding navigation policy and operational principles.

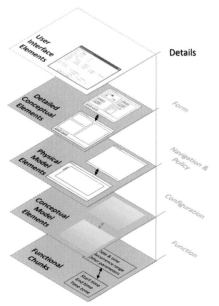

This book addresses primarily the layers and phases pertaining directly to the conceptual model and conceptual design. It does not address the detailed design aspects.

Summary of the Components of the Conceptual Model According to the Layered Framework

Let us put it all together. Specifically, summarize the three key aspects of the conceptual model: the functional chunks, the configuration of conceptual elements, and the navigation map and policy, for each of the four appointment setting applications analyzed earlier.

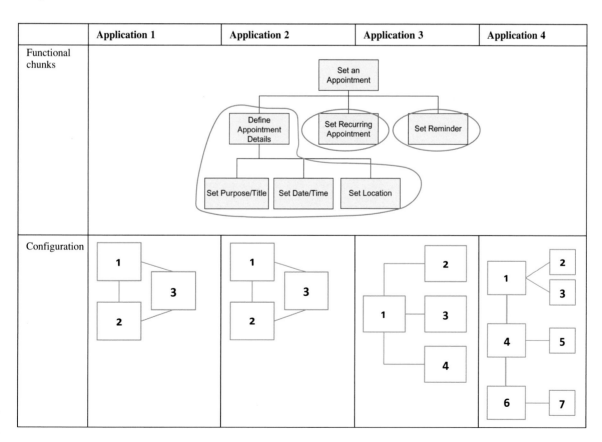

	Application 1	Application 2	Application 3	Application 4
Functional chunks				
Configuration				

Navigation and policy	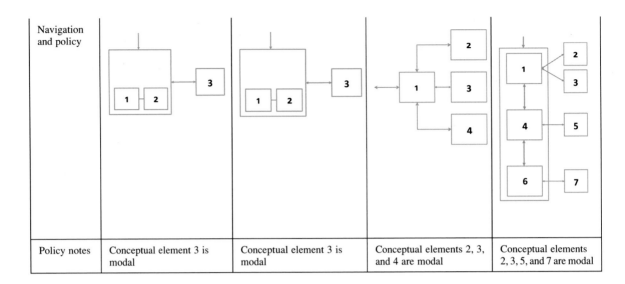			
Policy notes	Conceptual element 3 is modal	Conceptual element 3 is modal	Conceptual elements 2, 3, and 4 are modal	Conceptual elements 2, 3, 5, and 7 are modal

Conceptual Models Matter!: Implications to Human Performance, Usability, and Experience

Earlier in the book, after introducing the four calendar applications, we asked what the fundamental differences between them are. Moreover, do those fundamental differences matter? The discussion of the conceptual model using the layered framework addressed the first question in depth. However, what about the second question: do those differences matter? In order to discuss why the conceptual model matters, let us distinguish between "human performance," on the one hand, and "usability and user experience," on the other hand. Human performance refers to perceptual, cognitive, emotional, and physical processes and behaviors. Usability and user experience refer to the effectiveness, the efficiency, and the subjective experience associated with users interacting with an application in order to accomplish goals.

There are strong connections between human performance and usability. A simple example can illustrate this: assume that a user has difficulties in reading some information off a display. This is an issue with perception and possibly some cognitive aspects related to comprehension. Such a degraded perceptual and cognitive process could result in reduced effectiveness of the user's interaction with the application. Thus, human performance can directly affect usability and user experience.

The discussion of why conceptual models matter focuses on five fundamental human psychology and performance factors that play a role in any interaction. This focus illustrates how the configuration of functional chunks, "places," and "routes" underlying the UI can influence performance. The five factors are the following:

If you understand it, you can use it! The user interface of any interactive product or system should be such that we understand it. In order to understand, we need to develop and keep a mental representation of what we deal with—be it another person, a situation, an artifact they use, or an action they take. People construct mental structures, or mental models, to represent what they know. The mental structures typically consist of elements and the links between them. The elements could be words, concepts, images, names, places, episodes, experiences, and actions. A person's knowledge on a topic comprises elements and their links. Some links are strong; others are weak. When

Use these five human performance factors to assess implications of conceptual models:

- Mental models and understanding
- Location awareness
- Visual search effectiveness
- Operational (executing actions) load
- Working memory load

On Mental Models

Norman refers to one's understanding when interacting with an artifact as "having a conceptual model of the device you interact with" (Norman, 1983, 1988, 1999, 2004). The internal, psychological representation of this model is often referred to as the user's model or a mental model. To quote Norman's definition: "Mental models [are] the models people have of themselves, others, the environment, and the things with which they interact. People form mental models through experience, training, and instruction. The mental model of a device is formed largely by interpreting its perceived actions and its visible structure" (Norman, 1988, p. 17). Hollnagel (1988) suggested that a mental model is the operator's knowledge about his or her environment and is crucial for how the operator interprets, plans, and acts. Similarly to Norman, Hollnagel claimed that the operator's model of the world is shaped by how the world is presented. Young (1981) also suggested that users create mental representations of the system they work with and that this helps them plan their actions and understand the system's behavior. According to Moray (1987), users develop small working models of subcomponents of the system they interact with in order to reduce the mental workload that may be associated in that interaction. Taken together, these approaches to define mental models focus primarily on the representation of the device or system that the user interacts with and its environment.

interacting with an artifact, the user either starts with a preexisting mental structure about that artifact or constructs a new one based on the interaction and experience with the artifact. When one's preexisting mental structure corresponds with the structure of the artifact one interacts with, it is easier to understand. Alternatively, if a user does not have a preexisting mental structure, the artifact should convey a structure that will facilitate understanding and the construction of a corresponding mental structure. The configuration underlying the user interface is composed of functional chunks, "places," and "routes." It conveys information that users can utilize in constructing their mental representation and understanding better the product they interact with. The methodology part of the book will address the challenge of matching the conceptual model to users' mental models.

If you know where you are, you can get to your destination! The first thing we most likely do when interacting with a system is orient ourselves, that is, become aware of where we are. Next and also likely, we want to get to a destination, the "place" that contains the desired parameters and actions. As was emphasized earlier, "places" can be conceptual or physical. Different screens and windows in the interaction flow represent different physical "places" the user visits in order to accomplish a goal. These include finding parameters and actions, setting them, and/or executing them. For one to take the correct "route," get to the correct "place," and not "get lost," one needs good location awareness. Location awareness is about knowing which "place" one visited, the "place" one is at, and "places" that are yet to be visited. Having good location awareness increases the likelihood of getting to the correct "place" faster.

There are various factors that can influence location awareness, among which are the number of locations visited, the "landmarks" and "you are here" aids to orientation, and the length and complexity of routes between locations. Fewer "places," and consequently fewer "routes" among the "places," would be typically associated with better location awareness,

On Location Awareness

Location awareness is our ability to recognize where we are relative to what is around us, relative to the route we took to get to where we are, and relative to other places that could be destinations.

compared with many "places" and "routes." Location awareness may be more effective when navigating between conceptual "places" located in the same physical place in comparison with navigating between conceptual places, which are located in different physical places.

If you can find what you look for, you can accomplish your goal! Typically, when we start a task with a given goal, we will search for the functions and parameters relevant to executing the task and accomplishing the goal. We can search for clues to give us orientation. We can search for what will help us go to other places. Probably, one of the most common behaviors we engage with when reaching a "place" is to perform a visual search. Having an effective and efficient visual search means finding the correct "target" faster.

On Visual Search

Visual search is a perceptual process whereby we scan the visual scene and search for a given target. During such a process, any other non-target element in the scene is a distracter.

Visual search is influenced primarily by the amount of items in the scene and their specific visual attributes such as size, color, shape, and similarity to other items. The amount of items in any given physical place depends upon the determination of functional chunks and conceptual elements and the assignment of conceptual elements to physical places. Having more conceptual elements in the same physical place may support better location awareness, as was discussed above; however, it may also be a challenge for effective visual search. Conversely, having less conceptual elements in a given physical place may facilitate more effective visual search; however, it may also degrade location awareness.

It is important to note that even in a physical place with many conceptual elements, it is possible to facilitate visual search by proper visual layout and organization even with a large number of elements. However, the implications discussed here are directly related to the mere number of "places" based on functional chunking and if it results in a higher or lower number of elements in each physical place.

If you do fewer actions, your effort is reduced! The user executes actions as part of the interaction with the application. These could range from actions related to traveling from one "place" to another, to starting and concluding the tasks, to actions related to the setup of parameters. Executing actions is influenced by the amount and difficulty of actions required to perform the task and accomplish the goal. Having less and easier operations increases the likelihood of performing tasks more accurately and faster.

On Operational Load

Operational load is the mental or physical effort we invest when performing actions as part of our interaction with a product.

The issue of action difficulty when interacting with contemporary user interfaces typically involves movements of a pointing device (be it the hand and fingers or a mouse or a stylus) and pressing or clicking. These could be relatively easy to some user populations, but rather challenging to others (e.g., the aging population). The amount of required actions can vary as a function of conceptual elements and their assignment to physical places. Fewer physical places, and consequently fewer "routes" among the places, would be associated with fewer actions compared with many physical places and "routes." In other words, fewer physical places and "routes" would be associated with a reduced operational load.

On Working Memory

Working memory is a transient and limited-capacity memory buffer we use to store and retrieve information we require while performing actions and interacting with a product.

If you are not required to remember much, you can do more! Interaction is inherently sequential. We tend to do things one after another, and it is very challenging to do things simultaneously. To accomplish our goals, we should be fully aware of what we did and where, what we are doing now and where, and what we are yet to do and where. For this, we have to store the information about actions and "places" in some sort of a memory buffer. The psychology of perception, attention, and memory refers to this as working memory. The working memory is transient in the sense that it keeps for a relatively short time (4-10 s) and is limited in terms of the amount of information it can store and use at a given moment. Thus, having few steps and/or fewer "places" and "routes" in an interaction aimed at achieving a given goal implies less challenge/load to the duration and capacity of the working memory. Reduced load on the working memory increases the likelihood of performing tasks more accurately and efficiently.

Implications of the Conceptual Models of the Appointment Setup Examples to Human Performance

Now we can see how the different conceptual models of the four appointment applications matter to human performance. The following is a comparative analysis with four human performance parameters: location awareness, visual search, operational load, and working memory load. The potential impact of the mental model factor is not included in this analysis since it cannot be measured, particularly when user profile and persona are not considered. The second part of the book on the methodology of conceptual design considers this.

For the purpose of the comparison, we use a relative scale; that is, the ratings here are comparative among the four applications. They do not imply anything in absolute terms. In addition, the ratings are hypothetical and indicate a likelihood rather than something that is empirical. Finally, the ratings do not imply that any one of the four applications is "better" than any of the others. The analysis shows that the configuration underlying the user interface has implications to human performance.

There are two important conclusions to this analysis:

1. **The configuration can have an impact on human performance**. Based on the definitions and understanding of each of the four human performance factors and the possible influences on these factors, it seems that the mere configuration of

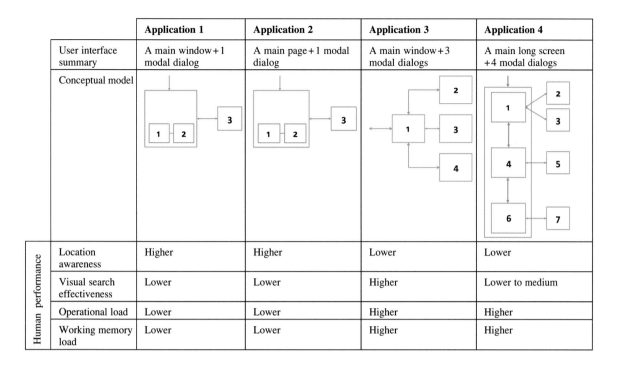

	Application 1	Application 2	Application 3	Application 4
User interface summary	A main window+1 modal dialog	A main page+1 modal dialog	A main window+3 modal dialogs	A main long screen +4 modal dialogs
Conceptual model				
Location awareness	Higher	Higher	Lower	Lower
Visual search effectiveness	Lower	Lower	Higher	Lower to medium
Operational load	Lower	Lower	Higher	Higher
Working memory load	Lower	Lower	Higher	Higher

(The left side of the lower rows is labeled "Human performance" vertically.)

"places" and "routes" underlying the UI of each of the four applications can have an impact on human performance. The impact for each of the four performance factors is different for each application and is associated with differences in the configuration.

2. **There are trade-offs among the human performance factors**. There seems to be a trade-off between location awareness and visual search effectiveness. Trade-offs are typical to human performance and thus pose a challenge when attempting to determine if a given interactive system is "better" than another with respect to human performance. Nevertheless, there are some trade-offs that may result in an overall better performance than other trade-offs. For example, in the analysis of the human performance implications of the four applications, application 1 has a high location awareness and low working memory load, whereas application 4 have a low location awareness and high working memory load. It is more likely that the overall resulting performance will be "better" with application 1 as compared with application 4. However, application 1 has a lower visual search effectiveness that may compensate for the other poorer performance factors in the overall performance relative to application 4. Figure 9.1 presents the hypothetical trade-offs in the basic human performance implications for the two applications.

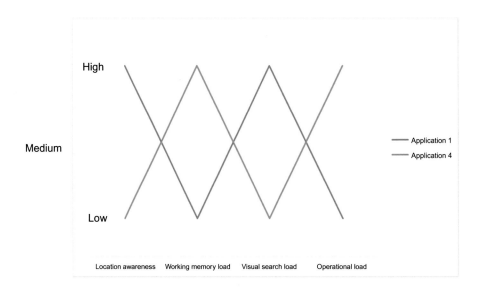

At this point, we should not attempt to resolve this challenge, but agree that the first and most important conclusion is **to be aware of the impact the underlying configuration can have on human performance**.

USABILITY AND USER EXPERIENCE IMPLICATIONS

The underlying configuration of the UI has an impact on its human performance factors. These, in turn, can have an impact on user experience. Here, we discuss four factors that are popular in the usability and user experience discipline:

Learnability: Learnability is the rate and ease by which a user learns to use the application. Many factors influence learning. For the purpose of the discussion here, we will focus on the mental load imposed primarily by working memory load.

Effectiveness: Effectiveness is the accuracy and completeness with which users achieve specific goals (ISO 9241-11). Location awareness and the effectiveness of the visual search heavily affect accuracy and completeness.

Efficiency: Efficiency is the resources expended in relation to the accuracy and completeness with which users achieve goals (ISO 9241-11). The more a task loads working memory, the more mental resources it costs to perform.

Satisfaction: In addition to effectiveness and efficiency, the third parameter of usability according to ISO 9241-11 is satisfaction, the comfort and acceptability of use.

Note that with the increased awareness and consideration of the more holistic aspects of user experience, we increasingly look at additional emotional aspects of interacting with products such as joy, fun, and engagement. When linking the human performance factors discussed above, we can assume that high location awareness, easy visual search, and low working memory load would be associated with better emotional aspects, satisfaction, joy, fun, and engagement.

Usability Implications of the Conceptual Models of the Appointment Examples

The following is a comparative analysis of the possible impact of the configuration of each of the four applications on the usability metrics. As before, for the purpose of the comparison, we use a relative scale; that is, the ratings here are comparative among the four applications. They do not imply anything in absolute terms. They also do not imply that any one of the four applications is "better" than the others. In addition, the ratings are hypothetical and indicate a likelihood rather than something that is empirical. The analysis in Table 9.1 shows that the configuration underlying the user interface affects usability and user experience.

TABLE 9.1:
Usability implications of the conceptual models of the four calendar applications

		Application 1	Application 2	Application 3	Application 4
	User interface summary	A main window + 1 modal dialog	A main page + 1 modal dialog	A main window + 3 modal dialogs	A main long screen + 4 modal dialogs
	Conceptual model				
Usability and user experience	Learnability	Higher	Higher	Medium	Lower
	Effectiveness	Medium	Medium to high	Medium	Medium
	Efficiency	Medium	Medium to high	Lower	Lower
	Satisfaction	Medium to high	Medium	Medium to high	Medium to high

The conclusions of this analysis are the following:

1. **The configuration can have an impact on usability and user experience**. Considering the human psychology and performance aspects, these in turn influence the nature of the interaction, that is, the usability and user experience. Since performance and usability are tightly linked, the decision which "places" to put elements in and the "routes" taking the user from one place to another impact usability as well.

2. **The impact can be context-sensitive**. When it comes to usability and user experience, user's profile is a critical factor in the nature of the interaction. The second part of the book on the methodology considers this factor.

A Typology of Conceptual Models

We have talked about conceptual models in general terms and illustrated them with the appointment applications. However, the illustrations showed us very specific models. Are there general types of models? In other words, can we talk about a typology of conceptual models? A typology can give us

1. general criteria for appropriateness of a model type to a given situation,
2. terms to compare between alternative models.

There are several published typologies of website architectures (Brinck, Gergle, & Wood, 2002; Garrett, 2002; Lynch & Horton, 2008). The following is a light adaptation of some of those typologies to conceptual models underlying any user interface, be it a website or any application and regardless if it is online or offline.

Conceptual models differ in the degrees of freedom given to the user in accomplishing tasks and achieving goals. In some cases, the task flow is highly structured and linear, thus giving the user less degrees of freedom in terms of alternative ways of the interaction. In other cases, the task flow is unstructured, thus giving the user more degrees of freedom in terms of alternatives in how to perform the interaction. Following this, typologies of conceptual models can be divided into two main categories:

1. Sequential and structured: including single-sequence and hierarchy or multiple-sequence models
2. Nonsequential and unstructured: including hub and spokes, matrix, and network models

A system rarely consists of a single model. Each of the following typologies is like a simple or a complex building block in a broader conceptual model that likely consists of a combination of several of these typologies. Most of the examples below illustrate how typical this is in most programs. "Hybrid Conceptual Models" at the end of this section discusses this.

SEQUENTIAL AND STRUCTURED MODELS

Single sequence

Configuration: Several conceptual elements configured in a linear sequence, with each element linked to the element leading to it and to the following conceptual model element in the sequence (Figure 10.1).

Conceptual navigation map: The single-sequence structure has a single entry point and a single exit/conclusion point. Navigation is possible only forward or backward within each pair of linked conceptual model elements in the sequence.

Navigation policy: Only a single conceptual model element is available for interaction at any given time.

Exceptions and variations: All or some of the conceptual model elements in the sequence have an exit, thus not forcing the user to go through all conceptual model elements in the sequence in order to exit the interaction.

Performance implications:

- Location awareness—high
- Visual search effectiveness—high
- Operational (executing actions) load—low
- Working memory load—low

Usability implications:

- Learnability—fast and easy
- Effectiveness—high
- Efficiency—low
- Satisfaction—likely high

Appropriate for:
The single-sequence model supports

- short task sequences,
- highly structured tasks (there is a prescribed order with which the user must perform and complete the task),
- infrequent tasks,
- tasks primarily for novices and users who need guidance,

FIGURE 10.1:
A schematic example for a single-sequence conceptual model.

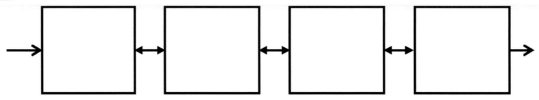

- when it is very important to prevent errors,
- where location awareness is important, and
- when users are otherwise distracted/interrupted/overloaded within the overall usage context.

With respect to devices, this conceptual model is appropriate for mobile and small-screen devices.

Example for a single-sequence model

The installation wizard for so many programs is a typical example for a single-sequence conceptual model. Note that in this example, the navigation map provides an exit point in every conceptual element. In addition, each conceptual element appears in a window of its own (Figure 10.2).

FIGURE 10.2:
An example for a single-sequence conceptual model.

Hierarchy or multiple sequences

Configuration: Several conceptual elements configured as a hierarchy, with a source "parent" element linked to several other "child" elements, and each subsequent element could be linked further to other "child" elements.

A hierarchical structure supports multiple sequences based on all possible branches in the hierarchy. Each sequence is ad hoc, as it were, and exists as a function of a specific interaction sequence the user performs in order to accomplish a goal. The example here (Figure 7.1, right-hand side) illustrates how the hierarchy supports two possible sequences.

Note that the relatively simple hierarchy in this figure can support up to six sequences, two of them consisting of two conceptual model elements and four with three conceptual model elements each (Figure 10.3).

Conceptual navigation map: A hierarchical structure has a single entry and exit point at the source "parent" element. It allows forward and backward navigation within each pair of linked elements. In order to conclude the interaction, the user is required to navigate back to the source element. From there, the user can either exit or initiate another interaction sequence.

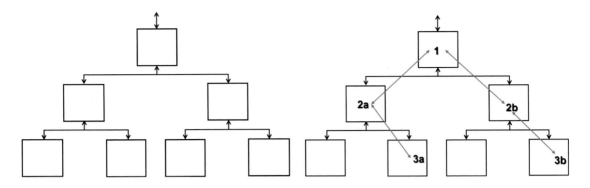

FIGURE 10.3:

A schematic example for a three-level hierarchical conceptual model (left) and two possible interaction sequences on the same model (right).

Interaction policy: Only a single conceptual element is available for interaction at any given time.

Exceptions and variations: All or some of the elements in the sequence have an exit, thus not forcing the user to go through all conceptual elements in the sequence in order to exit the interaction. Another exception/variation is having more than a single source or "parent" conceptual element.

Performance implications:

- Location awareness—medium
- Visual search effectiveness—high
- Operational (executing actions) load—low
- Working memory load—medium

Usability implications:

- Learnability—fast and easy
- Effectiveness—high
- Efficiency—low
- Satisfaction—likely medium to high

Appropriate for:

- Functional chunks that have logical and relevant hierarchical relations between them.
- There are several related user goals that are typically or ideally accomplished more or less at the same time.
- Efficiency and flexibility are not essential.
- Location awareness is critical.

With respect to devices, this conceptual model is appropriate for mobile and small-screen devices.

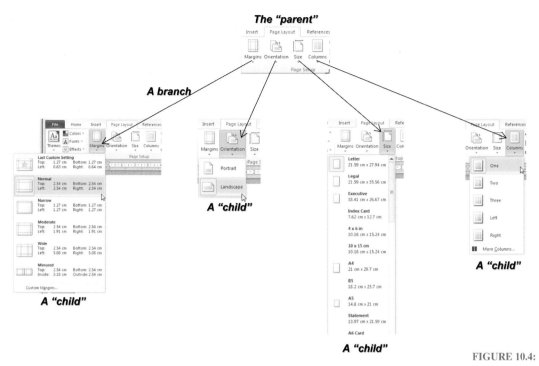

FIGURE 10.4:
An example for a hierarchy or multiple-sequence model.

Example for a hierarchy or multiple-sequence conceptual model

In this example, the "parent" element is a part of a much larger program. The "parent" or root element of the hierarchy is the starting point for navigating in several, mutually exclusive, routes leading to "child" conceptual elements. Each of those is modal, that is, it allows for the interaction with that element and then getting back to the "parent" level (Figure 10.4).

NONSEQUENTIAL AND UNSTRUCTURED MODELS

Hub and spokes

Configuration: The model consists of a primary and central conceptual element where most of the interaction takes place. The central element is linked to several elements where additional tasks are performed that are supplemental to the tasks performed in the central element.

Conceptual navigation map: The hub and spokes configuration has a single entry and exit point at the primary and central conceptual element. It allows the user to

FIGURE 10.5:
A schematic example for a hub and spokes conceptual model with the navigation map.

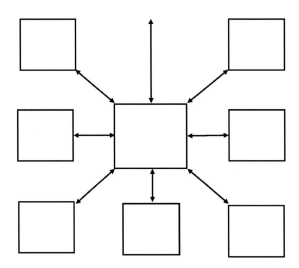

navigate to any of the supplemental elements, perform the task there, and return to the primary element.

Interaction policy: Some of the supplemental elements can be available for interaction at the same time that the user interacts with the central element, and some will not allow simultaneous interaction with the central element or with other supplemental elements (Figure 10.5).

Exceptions and variations: All or some of the elements in the configuration may have either exit points or links to other supplementary elements, aside from the link to the central element.

Performance implications:

- Location awareness—medium
- Visual search effectiveness—high
- Operational (executing actions) load—low
- Working memory load—medium

Usability implications:

- Learnability—fast and easy
- Effectiveness—high
- Efficiency—low
- Satisfaction—likely medium to high

Appropriate for:

- Functional chunks that have many parameters and actions (all of them should be together to support task completion)

- When the user tends to focus on one or several related main tasks most of the time and requires a single "place" to perform them
- When additional, local, and temporary tasks supplement the performance of those main tasks with little interruption to the main workflow

An example for a hub and spokes conceptual model

In this example, the hub is a window hosting a conceptual element consisting of parameters and actions pertaining to the definition of a style in a word processing program. While the hub can include many of the style definition tasks, there are supplementary elements to fine-tune the setup of parameters. Each of these supplemental elements is placed in a modal window allowing the conclusion of the fine-tune setup of the parameter and return to the hub before proceeding anywhere else (Figure 10.6).

FIGURE 10.6:
An example for a hub and spokes conceptual model.

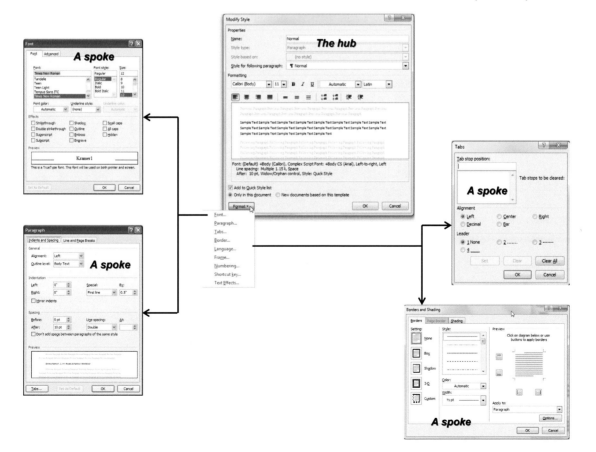

Matrix

Configuration: There are two key characteristics to the matrix conceptual model:

1. There are several and parallel starting points (in contrast to the sequential and structured models that have a single starting point).
2. There are at least two, related or independent, sets of such starting points. That is the reason it is named a matrix.

Visualizing this model as having two dimensions expresses the strategy of having parallel interaction flows. In a matrix configuration with two independent dimensions, there is no functional or interaction flow dependency between the elements in one dimension and the elements in the other. In a matrix configuration with two related dimensions, an interaction with a given element in one dimension will determine the available elements in the other dimension.

The two visualizations in Figure 10.7 reflect two common approaches to this model:

A. Each of the parallel starting points in each dimension leads to a sequence of linked conceptual elements.

FIGURE 10.7:
Two examples for a matrix conceptual model: A. Parallel, related or unrelated, starting points linked to a sequence or group of additional elements; B. Parallel, related or unrelated, starting points linked to a central element.

B. Each of the parallel starting points in each dimension leads to a single conceptual element where most of the interaction is taking place.

Conceptual navigation principles: There are multiple entry and exit points with no sequential dependency among them; the user can start at any of the points. Once the user enters an interaction flow at a given starting point, the relevant functional chunk or chunks may appear in a single place (B in Figure 10.7) that

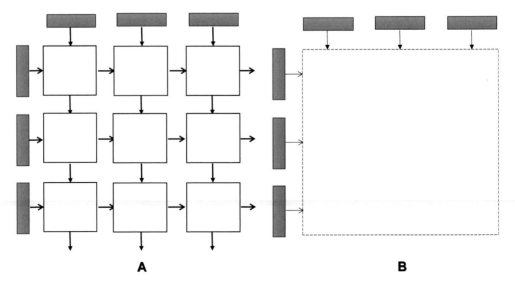

A   B

may include more than one conceptual element. Alternatively, entering an interaction flow at a given starting point may invoke several conceptual elements assigned to several physical places (A in Figure 10.7). The navigation among those can be as a single sequence or hub and spokes or, as will be discussed below, even a network-type navigation.

Interaction policy: The matrix model allows for interaction with more than one conceptual element at a time.

Performance implications:

- Location awareness—medium
- Visual search effectiveness—high to medium
- Operational (executing actions) load—low to medium
- Working memory load—medium

Usability implications:

- Learnability—medium
- Effectiveness—medium
- Efficiency—high
- Satisfaction—likely medium

Appropriate for:

- When there are clear sets of starting points that can be organized as different dimensions.
- When dependency between sets of starting points is relevant.
- When the overall task structure is such that there is no single start or end.
- When the user requires the flexibility and control to initiate different tasks and workflows depending on the objectives.
- There are parallel workflows with no particular order, importance, or priority among them.

An example for a matrix conceptual model

The example for a matrix conceptual model is a bank web. The site provides multiple starting points implemented as a horizontal row of tabs at the top of the page and the user can select any of those tabs at any time. There are additional parallel starting points available once the user made a selection in the horizontal dimension of the matrix. These two dimensions are dependent. Once the user makes the subsequent selection in the vertical set of starting points, the relevant conceptual element becomes available in the center of the page (similar to option B in Figure 10.7).

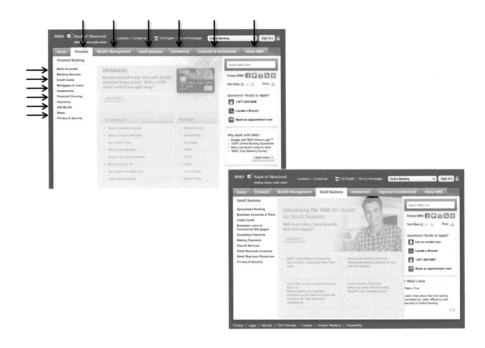

The implementation of the matrix concept does not necessitate a literal translation to the visual appearance; that is, both dimensions do not have to visually appear as two orthogonal sets of options. It is possible to have both sets, the two dimensions of the matrix, to appear as two horizontal sets of options, and these could represent dependent and independent sets (Figure 10.8).

Network

Conceptual configuration: The model consists of multiple entry points and multiple interlinked conceptual elements and physical places. The configuration provides the user with many degrees of freedom with respect to where to start interaction flow and where to navigate. Almost by definition, many websites have a fundamental network conceptual model underlying their architecture (Figure 10.9).

Conceptual navigation principles: The user can initiate multiple interaction flows from multiple starting points. Since there are multiple links between conceptual elements, the user can navigate to some destinations in more than one route. In addition, the user may start on a given route and deviate to a different route without necessarily concluding the initial one. The user can exit at various points as well.

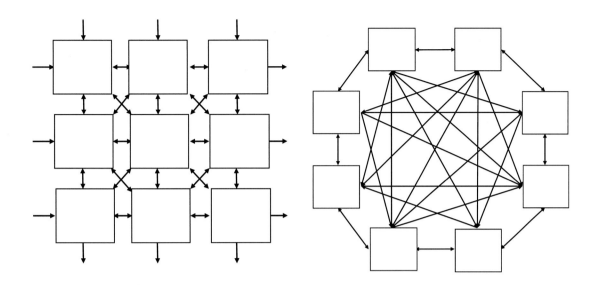

FIGURE 10.9:
Two schematic depictions of a network conceptual model.

Interaction policy: The user can interact with more than one conceptual element at a time.

Performance implications:

- Location awareness—low
- Visual search effectiveness—high to medium
- Operational (executing actions) load—low to medium
- Working memory load—medium to high

Usability implications:

- Learnability—low to medium
- Effectiveness—medium to high
- Efficiency—high
- Satisfaction—medium

Appropriate for:

- When the overall task structure is such that there is no single start or end.
- When the user requires the flexibility and control to initiate different tasks and workflows depending on the objectives.
- When the user needs the ability to navigate to various places not necessarily related directly to a given workflow.
- There are parallel workflows with no particular order, importance, or priority among them.

An example for a network conceptual model

The example for a network conceptual model is the website of a commercial airline. The website has multiple conceptual elements in multiple pages. The example in Figure 10.10 highlights the multiple navigation routes the user can take to reach the same destination page. In order to navigate from the home page to the Delayed Flights & Cancellations page (route 1 in Figure 10.10), the user can select the Information & Services option in the home page (A in Figure 10.10) leading to the Information & Services page (B in Figure 10.10). In that page, the user can select the Delayed Flights and Cancellations option and navigate (route 2 in Figure 10.10) to the Delayed Flights & Cancellations page (C in Figure 10.10). Another way of reaching the Delayed Flights & Cancellations page is by selecting the Cancelled Flights Service option in the home page (route 3 in Figure 10.10).

FIGURE 10.10:
An example for a network conceptual model.

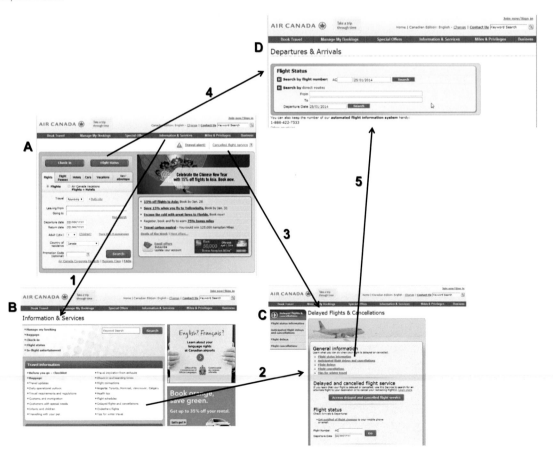

Another example is the navigation to the Flight Status page (D in Figure 10.10). One immediate option for doing this is available in the home page, which leads directly to the Flight Status page (route 4 in Figure 10.10). Another route is from the Delayed Flights & Cancellations page, by selecting the Flight Status option in that page (route 5 in Figure 10.10).

Hybrid conceptual models

It is rare to find any of the above model typologies as the single and exclusive model underlying any stand-alone application. In most cases, the conceptual model is a hybrid of several of the typologies outlined here. For example, an application could include an installation component based on a single-sequence conceptual model and then a hierarchy model for initiating several possible workflows, with each leading to a hub and spoke model for specific tasks. Constructing such hybrid models requires careful consideration of the appropriateness to user profiles and tasks. The relevance of hybrid models will be discussed in the methodology part of the book.

IS THERE A GOOD OR A BAD CONCEPTUAL MODEL? INTRODUCING CONCEPTUAL MODEL COMPLEXITY

It is very tempting to ask if there is such a thing as a "good" conceptual model. Is one type of a conceptual model better than another? The obvious answer is: it depends. A more reasonable question is which model or combination of models is more appropriate for a given context/task/user. Part of the above overview of each model typology looked into this question, specifically in the section addressing what each model type is appropriate for. Now, to take this discussion further, we examine the idea of conceptual model complexity.

Let us start with a basic assumption: Complex conceptual models are not bad, and simple conceptual models are not always good. Rather, **a conceptual model is as good as it supports the context/goal/task/user**. The key characteristics that may influence model complexity and their relations are presented in Figure 10.11. The various models differ primarily in the extent with which they support the level of task structuredness (the horizontal axis in Figure 10.11). Tasks and workflows can be highly structured in terms of the sequence of required steps and the minimization of decision points and navigation branching introduced along the way. As simple things go, the more structured the task, the more effectiveness is afforded. Supporting the task structuredness goes hand in hand with the amount of degrees of freedom the conceptual

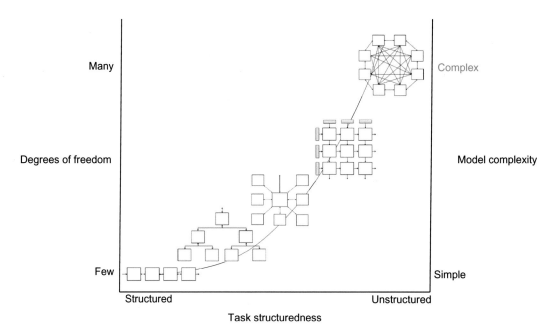

Many

Degrees of freedom

Few

Complex

Model complexity

Simple

Structured

Unstructured

Task structuredness

FIGURE 10.11:
A summary and comparative view of the conceptual model typologies as a function of the level of structuredness of the tasks it supports, the degrees of freedom each provides, and the resulting complexity of the model.

model provides the user in accomplishing tasks and achieving goals (the left-hand vertical axis in Figure 10.11). This is typically reflected in the number of conceptual elements, the number of entry and exit points, and the number of possible routes a user can take. The more degrees of freedom the model provides, the more flexibility and control are afforded in performing a variety of tasks and workflows. This often results in higher efficiency, particularly beneficial for experienced and expert users. The network model offers the user more degrees of freedom in comparison to the single-sequence model. The single-sequence model is supportive and appropriate for tasks that are highly structured in comparison with the network model.

Simply put, complexity is a system or a situation consisting of many elements interlinked in many diverse ways. Characterizing the models in terms of the degrees of freedom they provide and the task structuredness they support has implications to model complexity. A model that supports a highly structured task with fewer degrees of freedom is a simpler model. A model that supports unstructured tasks with more degrees of freedom is a more complex model. The curve connecting the different models in Figure 10.11 implies that the relation between level of task structuredness and degrees of freedom, on the one hand, and resulting complexity of the model, on the other hand, is not necessary linear. In other words, the increase in model complexity can be somewhat accelerated as the model provides more and more degrees of freedom to support tasks that are less and less structured.

As stated at the beginning of this section, a conceptual model is as good as it supports the context/goal/task/user. On the one hand, the more complex the model is, the more likely it will be harder for the users to understand them and this may impact learning, usability, and overall experience. However, this does not imply in any way that complex conceptual models are bad. Complex conceptual models support unstructured task flows and can be appropriate for experienced and expert users.

Do not ask: what is a "good" conceptual model? The methodology part of this book is all about the question you should ask: given the context/goal/task/user, what is the "best" conceptual model that can support it?

Summary of Part 1

This part of the book analyzed and discussed the concept of conceptual model and its significance to performance and usability. These are your take-aways:

- The conceptual model is composed of functional chunks and their respective conceptual elements, the configuration of the conceptual elements, the assignment of conceptual element to physical places, a navigation map among the elements, and a navigation policy.
- There are several typologies of conceptual models: sequence, hierarchy, hub and spokes, matrix, and the network. Typically, however, most applications have a conceptual model that is a hybrid of these typologies.
- Different conceptual models differ in the amount of degrees of freedom provided to the user in meeting the structuredness of the task. This in turn can result in varying degrees of model complexity.
- The conceptual model has implications to human performance, usability, and experience. With respect to performance, the conceptual model impacts understanding of the product and how to work with it (mental models), location awareness while interacting, the effectiveness of visual search, operational load, and working memory load.

Conceptual Design: A Methodology

This part of the book introduces a step-by-step methodology for developing the conceptual model for interactive systems. It is advisable to read the first part of the book to get an overview of what a conceptual model is. However, this part revisits the framework for conceptual design and the key ideas and concepts relevant to the process. So you can go right ahead and start here to follow the methodology and design your conceptual model.

Conceptual Design in Context: Think Strategically

Involvement in conceptual design requires you to have good strategic awareness and to leverage that awareness in the conceptual design process. What is the meaning of having strategic awareness? Simply put, it means being aware of the larger context within which the conceptual design takes place. This chapter discusses some aspects of strategic awareness and thinking and their relevance to conceptual design.

THE BUSINESS CONTEXT: MOTIVATIONS FOR DEVELOPING THE PRODUCT AND VALUE PROPOSITIONS

When we design the user interface, we naturally consider user and usage aspects. But that is not all. The strategic and business side of things has a huge impact on how a product is designed and developed and, consequently, has an impact on usability and user experience. Being aware of the strategic and business aspects includes addressing questions such as the following: Is the product a revision and update of an existing product? Alternatively, is it a completely new product, perhaps based on new technology?

An update for an existing product puts the designer and developer in a context where there is some experience with the product, there is a user population that can be accessed in user research, the stronger and weaker aspects of the product are known or at least can be researched via summative usability testing, and a style has been set for the user interface and interaction with the product. In contrast, if it is a completely new product, there is no coherent and accessible user population, there is much uncertainty with respect to what maybe the strong and weak aspects of the product, and user interface and interaction styles are to be defined.

However, here is a cautionary note: It may sound as if the designer's life is easier with a revision or update of an existing product compared with a new product. This is not necessarily so and there is a downside to the benefits. An existing product may carry over a legacy that constrains the revision or an update work, constrain that does not exist with a new product. In contrast, a new product can introduce many uncertainties that may result in uninformed design decisions.

As a designer, you must know why a product is developed, be it a new one or a revision and update. You must be aware of the motivation and fully understand its value proposition for the end user and other stakeholders. Such understanding and awareness provide you with information that should be applied in the design to facilitate meeting the goals and objectives dictated by the motivation.

There could be various reasons to update or revise a product or develop a new product. Let us have a quick glance at the most common ones:

Meeting user needs—An existing user population may have previously unmet or new needs. These can be uncovered via venues such as requests, complaints, frequency and nature of using support and help facilities, ongoing usability testing, and user surveys. Uncovering those needs can define new directions for either updating existing products or developing new ones.

Providing new or improved technology—The discovery and development of a new technology, be it hardware- or software-based, is very often a major catalyst in developing a new product or in revising and updating an existing product. The discovery and development of a new technology could be as a response to user needs or a serendipitous outcome of unrelated processes and developments. In those cases, where new technology emerges and it might not relate to user needs, it is the role of interaction and UX designers to uncover the relevant user needs and design according to those. It is the social responsibility of all involved to ensure that the new technology is beneficial and does not or will not have any adverse impact on people and society.

Generating or increasing revenue—The motivation for developing a product is often the motivation for generating new revenue or increasing already existing revenue. Or in other words, follow the money. It is important to note that developing a new product or updating an existing product as a response to user needs is usually associated with generating and increasing revenue—either by getting new customers and clients and users or by retaining existing ones.

Other nonrevenue-related motivations—Not everything is driven by a desire for revenue. There are nonrevenue motivations such as social and environmental concerns. Any website or application serving a nonprofit organization is most likely driven by motivations and goals of that organization and not revenue-oriented goals. Any website or application supporting the service of a government to its citizens is not driven by revenue-oriented goals (at least not directly). It is usually aimed at informing, educating, and facilitating good citizenship.

Meeting business development, branding, and marketing opportunities—New business opportunities, some of which are related to responding to user needs, can be a driver for developing a product. Such opportunities arise with new technologies, new investments, new partners, and new competitions, local and global financial and market changes and fluctuations, and social and political changes. Any of those could influence business directions. Such directions can sometimes be associated with brand changes.

A designer must be aware and understand such changes and trends and include them as part of the design considerations.

THE DESIGN AND DEVELOPMENT CONTEXT: THE USER-ORIENTED APPROACH

Before diving into the methodology of conceptual design, let us put it into the design and development context. Conceptual design, while critical, is but one ingredient in the much larger context of designing, developing, and deploying interactive products. We assume you are familiar with designing for usability and user experience. Consequently, the following brief overview is only meant to establish common ground. It is not meant as a comprehensive or not even an introductory review of various approaches to the processes in the user interface and experience design.

The process with which we design and develop interactive systems has many definitions, prescriptions, standards, approaches, depictions, and visualizations. Most approaches follow similar core principles of the user-oriented design philosophy. The user-oriented approach has the simple yet powerful notion of having the user as the pivotal point of all activities. In addition, it advocates continuous involvement of all stakeholders—primarily the end user—and the iterative nature of the process involving the practice of early prototyping, evaluations and testing, redesigning, and retesting. Thus, if we transcend above a specific approach, the process of designing the user interface of interactive systems typically consists of several generic activities. These generic activities share the aim of impacting user experience, both in utility and in emotional aspects. These are presented briefly here in the typical order they can be performed (Figure 11.1), but this presentation of activities and their order is not meant to be prescriptive at all.

Conceptual models and conceptual design have been addressed throughout the years from diverse perspectives. Conceptual design is often viewed as a step or phase in-between doing some user research and deriving requirements and the detailed design of the system or program. Most of the treatment of conceptual design has been in the context of website design, focusing primarily on the challenge of designing effective information architecture. For example, Garrett (2002) discussed navigation models in information architecture, Lynch and Horton (2008) presented information architectures and navigation models, and Brinck, Gergle, and Wood (2002) discussed information architectures.

However, are conceptual models and conceptual design relevant only to the information architecture of websites? Norman (1983) referred to one's understanding when interacting with any artifact as "having a conceptual model of the device you interact with." He further suggested that conceptual models underlie the user interface linking between users' mental models about the artifact they interact with and how the artifact is designed and works. This implies a very important and critical role for the conceptual model for any system or product or computer program. It applies to anything the human user interacts with.

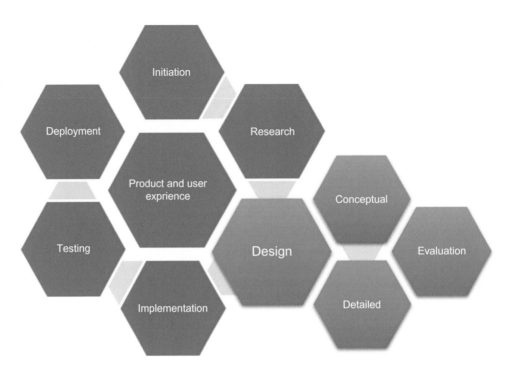

FIGURE 11.1:

The conceptual design activity in the overall context of designing user interfaces. The depiction here highlights the affinity with user research, on the one hand, and the transition to detailed design, on the other hand, with ongoing evaluation.

Initiation: Developing an interactive product and releasing it to users start with a need, an idea, a business opportunity, or a technological innovation. Regardless of the motivation and originating drive for the product, there is typically a primary phase that triggers all activities related to developing and releasing the product. This phase may include market research and needs assessment, development of business partnerships, technology assessment, and establishment of the project team. The latter is highly relevant to the design for UX because the team composition may influence the subsequent activities such as research and design.

Research: Research activities can be associated with the initiation phase and are often the basis for defining what should go into the product. This may include market and user research. User research is particularly critical for the design activities of the product. Some research activities can be revisited at later phases to gather more data or redo some of the analyses. Typically, the outcome of the initial user research is a set of requirements, some of which are the basis for the design activities. In this book, we put a lot of emphasis on the criticality of preliminary user research to design activities.

Design: The actual formulation of the user interface and implications for usability and user experience is realized through a series of design activities. This book focuses on the conceptual design activity within this context (Figure 11.1). The approach here advocates that user research and requirements are the basis for conceptual design, which then leads into detailed design. Evaluation and testing is an ongoing activity throughout both conceptual and detailed design.

Implementation: Once the design reaches a point where it can be implemented, the actual development and building of the product (e.g., code writing in a computer program) takes place. In some approaches (e.g., agile), design, testing, and implementation often overlap.

Testing: User-oriented approaches advocate early and frequent formative evaluation and testing that take place throughout the process. There are some cases where summative evaluation and testing take place before releasing the product to the end user. In some approaches, the testing is part of smaller and shorter cycles including design, implementation, and testing.

Deployment: The final phase, regardless of the development approach, is the release of the product to the end user and the initial or ongoing user support.

Depending on the approach and methodology of system development, these activities may take place in different orders. For example, some summative testing can take place at earlier stages of the process for parts of the product to be released; the product may be incomplete before release (such as in agile and lean approaches, where design and implementation and deployment can take place for parts of the system) or be highly iterative (e.g., research and redesign can be done after testing or lessons learned from deployment). Regardless of the specific approach, most do include all the core activities and processes described above.

Strategic and business considerations are intertwined in the overall human-oriented design and whatever specific design and development approach is taken. In addition, specific characteristics of project management are important to consider within the overall context of conceptual design. The following two sections address these issues.

PROJECT MANAGEMENT

The various business considerations and all the stakeholders influence managing the design and development enterprise as an effective project. As a designer, you should be concerned with (1) the ability to conduct user research within the development approach, (2) keeping the design priorities within the project, and (3) considering all the stakeholders that may have an impact on interaction and UX design.

Design and development approach: the place of user research

User and usage research are a prerequisite for the conceptual design of any product. In the classical and more traditional approaches of user-centered or human-oriented design, having conducted user research is an obvious step. Some of the more recent approaches such as the agile and lean approaches are more of a challenge to adequate user research because of their commitment to supply the end client/customer with an outcome as early as possible. Thus, spending time in up-front user research may seem by some as a waste of time, rather than a critical investment. Moreover, the work associated with the up-front development of the conceptual model fundamentals could also be seen as time that should rather be invested in actual development. Other published work provides some great ideas and perspectives on the place and role of designing for positive UX and usability in agile and lean development processes (Gothelf & Seiden, 2013; Ratcliffe & McNeill, 2012). The methodology outlined here assumes that some user and usage research have been conducted prior to embarking upon any of the design and development activities.

Multi- and cross-channel design and development strategy

Systems and products are designed and developed in such a way that they can run on multiple devices in multiple contexts. Moreover, users can start a task on one device and continue and/or complete the task on another device. This is referred to as multichannel or cross-channel interaction and experience, where channel is defined as the venue through which a user interacts with the subject matter or content domain of the application/product/system. In the computerized interactive systems realm, a channel is most often a device such as a desktop computer, a mobile device, an information booth or kiosk, an interactive voice response system, or any embedded interactive device (e.g., in-vehicle built-in navigation system).

The priorities within the project with respect to designing user interface, interaction, and UX for the various channels—when relevant—are set as a function of the business considerations. Updating an existing product due to user needs or new technology or other business goals and considerations could be realized in the form of adding a new channel. The design and development of that channel will thus get the highest priority in such a context. In a context of a new product aimed to be realized on several channels, priority can be given to one channel over others due to user needs or other business goals and considerations (e.g., competition and market needs and new partners).

The teamwork approach

Whatever the design and development approach is, a multidisciplinary team approach is critical for ensuring the effective inclusion of usability and UX considerations throughout the life cycle of the product. Moreover, it is critical for usability and UX design professionals to perform their task effectively. Usability and UX design professionals must work with users or user representatives. In addition, team up with other professions such as business, marketing, sales, engineering, software developers, graphic and industrial designers, and technical writers. Finally, and maybe indirectly, work with other stakeholders such as business partners, investors, and other providers to take into consideration their goals and concerns.

Conceptual Design: An Overview of the Methodology

REVISITING THE FRAMEWORK

The conceptual model was presented in the first part of the book within a layered framework. The layers underlie the final and detailed user interface. Building the conceptual model is the process of conceptual design and is at the heart of the methodology presented here in the second part of the book.

Taking the framework as the basis for the conceptual design process, there are three main phases to it from the bottom up (see Figure 12.1):

The conceptual design—This phase is the core of the methodology and spans three layers of the framework: the function, configuration, and the navigation and policy layers.

The transition from conceptual to detailed design—This is the phase where we transform the abstract aspects of the conceptual model to more concrete ones by adding details to them.

The detailed design—This is typically the final phase in designing the user interface, but it will not be covered in this book as it is focused on the conceptual design part of the entire process. While this represents activities beyond the conceptual design, it is in the framework because the conceptual model is the foundation for the final detailed design. In addition, detailed design is a significant part of the overall context of designing interactive systems.

The methodology will guide you through a series of design activities following the layers of the framework from the bottom up. First, we must address user research. We cannot, and should not, start the design process without having done some user research. With that in mind, we start in Chapter 13 with a refresher of some user research techniques and data types that are relevant to the conceptual design. Chapter 14 tells us how to determine the functional chunks and their interrelations. The next step in Chapter 15 is transforming the functional chunks into conceptual elements and linking between them to create the foundation of the model, the configuration of the elements. In Chapter 16, we take the model further and define the navigation map. Then, we fine-tune the navigation map in Chapter 17 by defining the navigation policy along with the assignment of conceptual elements to physical places. Finally, Chapter 18 covers the transition from the conceptual design activities towards detailed design. Each of the chapters will also provide some project management considerations.

FIGURE 12.1:
The layered framework of the conceptual model along with the design phases from conceptual design to the final detailed design.

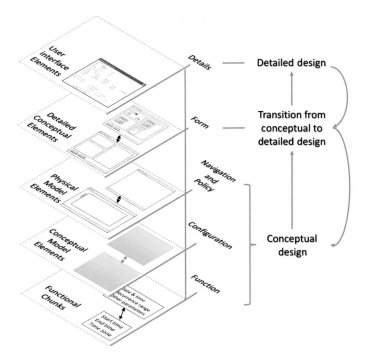

PROJECT MANAGEMENT CONSIDERATIONS: THIS DOES NOT HAVE TO BE A LINEAR PROCESS!

The process seems linear and you may doubt its applicability in some instances. Even though the process is described in a linear fashion, it is not to say that it is indeed linear. In other words, don't panic! It is not suggesting that we follow the infamous waterfall approach. But in the same vein, it is not to say that we necessarily follow an agile or lean approach. And as you will see, each step advocates an iterative process: revisiting previous steps and doing revisions.

The goal is not necessarily to follow a linear process but rather ensure that all layers of the design are covered and well integrated at the end.

First, User Research. Just Do It

Understanding key factors in user psychology and human performance is critical to the design of the conceptual models and their evaluation. To remind you, these factors include the following:

- Mental models and understanding
- Location awareness
- Visual search effectiveness
- Operational (executing actions) load
- Working memory load

User and usage research conducted before, during, and after the design can provide information and insights regarding those factors. As was said in the preface, familiarity with user and usage research is a prerequisite for this book. Since user research is critical to conceptual design, we will go over it here within a limited scope because the book focuses on the procedural steps in building the conceptual model. The following is a brief overview of some of the key techniques and outcomes in user research that are relevant to conceptual design. This overview will also introduce our "running" example for the methodology part of the book.

User and usage research, for whatever purpose it is, typically consist of the following:

- Data collection
- Analysis

DATA COLLECTION

Data sources and collection techniques

When conducting user and usage research, you want to get as close as possible to the real users and to the natural context where they perform their tasks and interactions. This will result in data that are closer to real life or, in more scientific words, have a higher ecological validity. However, sometimes, we have to compromise and conduct

TABLE 13.1:
A summary of the most common data sources and collection techniques in user research for design purposes

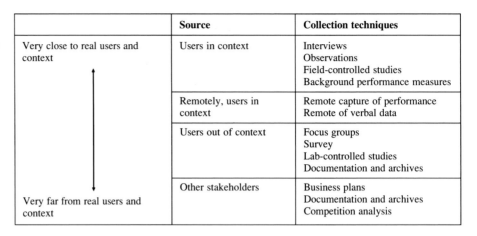

	Source	Collection techniques
Very close to real users and context	Users in context	Interviews Observations Field-controlled studies Background performance measures
	Remotely, users in context	Remote capture of performance Remote of verbal data
	Users out of context	Focus groups Survey Lab-controlled studies Documentation and archives
Very far from real users and context	Other stakeholders	Business plans Documentation and archives Competition analysis

the research away from the natural context or even not with the real users. Nevertheless, even with such distance, we can still collect valuable data that are highly relevant to the conceptual design process. Above is a brief overview of the most common data collection techniques in user research organized by our closeness to the real users and the natural context of usage (Table 13.1).

Data collected

The primary objective of data collection in user research is to have as much information as possible about users. Table 13.2 outlines the key research questions we would like answered. The most common data types, collected with the variety of collection

TABLE 13.2:
Data types as a function of research questions, along with key practical outcomes

		Data types				
		Qualitative	Quantitative			
		Verbal data and narratives	Counts and frequencies	Rating scales	Times and durations	Practical outcomes
Your research question	Who are the users?	✓	✓			User profiles and personas
	What do they do or want to do?	✓	✓	✓		Goals and tasks; subject-matter objects
	Why do they do what they do or want to do?	✓	✓	✓		Stories, scenarios, use cases
	In what context do they do it or want to do it?	✓	✓		✓	Places, times, states, and modes
	How do they do it?	✓	✓		✓	Interaction flows, task models, object-action maps

techniques outlined in the previous section, are listed along with the research questions. Finally, the table lists the practical outcomes of the data that provide answers to the questions and are utilized in the conceptual design.

ANALYSIS

The practical outcomes of various analyses of the data are answers to our research questions. The following is an overview of the key outcomes relevant to conceptual design. We also use this overview to introduce our "running" example for illustrating the conceptual design methodology. Our "running" example is literally an example about running. More specifically, it is about using devices and interactive applications aimed at facilitating and supporting the running experience.

User profiles and personas

Guided by both business goals and objectives, on the one hand, and the findings of the data collected, on the other hand, the existing or prospective user population is segmented into subpopulations. Each such segment constitutes a user profile and is uniformly characterized by the answers to the key research questions. Each segment is then represented by a persona. Various questions such as by which criteria to segment the population, how many user profiles and personas should be constructed, and what are the useful parameters of a persona are discussed in detail in other resources (Mulder & Yaar, 2007; Pruitt & Adlin, 2006). An example of a persona from our running example is presented in Figure 13.1.

User and usage scenarios

Scenarios are stories about users. Each persona has several such stories. Scenarios range from "cradle-to-grave" type stories covering the entire life cycle of users and a given product, to specific "A day in the life of…" stories, to very specific instances of interacting with the product. The scenario, as is in any good story, should provide background for the persona uncovering goals, intentions, motivations, states before, during, and after interacting with the product, outcomes, and consequences of the interaction, cognitions, actions, and feelings (Rosson & Carroll, 2009). You should have at least three scenario types for each persona:

1. A full life cycle scenario
2. A specific "day in the life"
3. A "problematic" scenario

   The scenarios serve as the primary foundation for performing subsequent analysis such as task and interaction flow analysis, object-action analysis, and journey and experience mapping.

Jake

"Running is like a movie. I see frames and build a story line from them"

General information

- Journalist
- Works with photographers and the editor
- Works 7 days a week, sometimes late at night
- Prefers in-city running, anytime
- Uses GPS and music player
- Heavy user of a smart phone

Jake is a journalist, working almost 24/7, living in Ottawa, Canada, and loves to run anytime, summer or winter. When he moved to Ottawa and wanted to run in the winter, he learned that he should put on layers, including heavy-duty gloves. Jake loves running with a heart rate (HR) monitor, a running tracking program that plays music, and always has his phone with him. He finds that having the running tracking program helps monitor his progress and decide if and how to change his workouts to keep on improving.

Goals

- Improve cardio
- Enjoy running

Amatuer

(radar chart with axes: Domain, Tech, Complexity, Human Env., Train, Attitude, Satisfaction, Pain points; scale 0, 2, 4, 6, 8)

Values

- Efficiency
- Hard work
- Aesthetics

Pain points

- Device setup
- Too many steps
- Info while running

FIGURE 13.1:
An example of a persona in the "running" example.

Persona and scenario implications

Let us consider the implications of the persona and the scenarios to the conceptual model. The persona reveals a very busy person with his occupation, yet passionate about running and highly motivated to keep and improve his physical shape. The persona seems to be tech-savvy and on the lookout for the state-of-the-art devices and applications as part of his running passion. Thus, he will most likely use the application if it fits his needs and habits.

The example scenario in Figure 13.2 reveals the very important aspect of multichannel and cross channel interactions. Designing for multichannel and cross channel interactions is a prevalent challenge and is very relevant to the focus of this book, conceptual design. As you will see soon, all examples from here on make the distinction between the channels, desktop and mobile, and the implications to the various activities and to the outcomes of the conceptual design process.

Task and workflow analysis

Users' interactions with a product consist of actions often referred to as tasks. You can perform user task analysis as a part of a job analysis, developing personnel

Jake is a journalist, working almost 24/7, living in Ottawa, Canada, and loves to run anytime, summer or winter. When he moved to Ottawa and wanted to run in the winter, he learned that he should put on layers, including heavy-duty gloves. Jake loves running with a heart rate (HR) monitor, a running tracking program that plays music, and always has his phone with him. He finds that having the running tracking program helps monitor his progress and decide if and how to change his workouts to keep on improving.

Jake researched the market and decided on using the iMRunning app in his iPhone, with a Bluetooth connection to the HR monitor, in order to have everything he likes in a single device. Jake set up a personal account through the iMRunning website on his desktop computer, which later linked and synchronized with the account on the mobile app.

When running in reasonable weather, Jake could easily setup the sensors and the app to connect and work. In addition, Jake prepared several workout plans that included defining parameters such as routes, distances, desired pace, and playlists. Every time he prepared to run, he would select one of the workout plans and then start. While running, he looks at his location and performance in terms of HR, distance, time, and speed by browsing the iMRunning app.

When done with the run, he had no trouble syncing the workout to his web account. He would always review the full details of the recent run, compare them with previous runs, and he even join a group through the iMRunning website on the desktop computer to both review and share running experiences with others. However, when running in subzero weather, with his gloves on, he had serious trouble with the setup. In addition, while running, he could not touch and browse the app on his iPhone. He had a serious problem using the app and the sensors when running in the dead of winter.

selection, training design, human-machine interface design and evaluation, or risk management and human error analysis. Task analysis is a family of techniques covering information gathering on user tasks, the analysis of the tasks, and producing results such descriptive lists, tables, diagrams, and narratives (e.g., Annett, 2004; Diaper & Stanton, 2004; Hackos & Redish, 1998; Kirwan & Ainsworth, 1992; Rosson & Carroll, 2002; Shepherd, 2000). However, the gathered information and its descriptive analysis are often not sufficient to meet the goals and objectives for the analysis. For example, the descriptive analysis of tasks of a bank teller may indicate that there is a major task of deposit, which is broken down into several subtasks. Such a descriptive analysis does not necessarily provide the designer with sufficient information on how this major task and its subtasks are to be represented in the user interface and if and how they are to be combined or integrated with other tasks.

The most common analysis used is hierarchical task analysis (HTA), where a hierarchy of tasks and subtasks represents the task structure. This approach is very popular because a hierarchy can represent many task structures, but note that sometimes tasks and subtasks do not necessarily have hierarchical relationships. The first step in the analysis is mapping the task structure. In other words, identify and define the top-level user goals, the various actions and events that the user does, and triggers that enable the achievement of the goals. In addition, when doing the

FIGURE 13.2:
An example for a full scenario—the running experience, part of the "running" example.

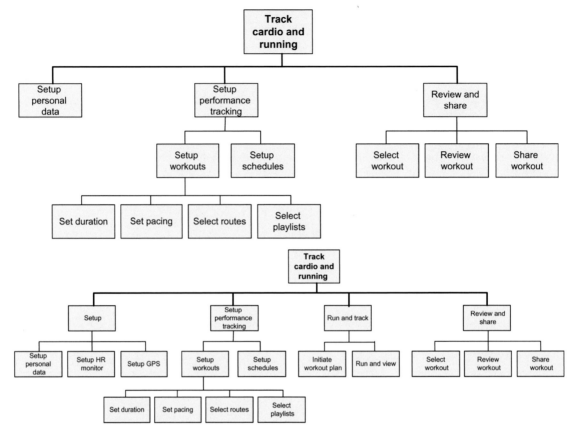

FIGURE 13.3:

An example for a hierarchical task analysis for the running example. The top diagram is the HTA for the desktop interaction channel, and the bottom diagram is the HTA for the mobile interaction channel.

"lean" version of HTA, focus on characteristics of tasks such as their frequency and difficulty.

The HTA of our running example presented in Figure 13.3 consists of two hierarchical task structures, one for the desktop interaction channel and the other for the mobile interaction channel. Similarly, two workflows of the running example are presented in Figure 13.4, one for each channel.

Object-action analysis

As part of the interactions with products, users manipulate or interact with various entities. These invariably appear in any story and user scenario. We refer to these entities as objects, and the user can perform various actions with any of those objects. Object-action analysis maps the interrelations among objects and their associated actions. This mapping is critical because any of these objects should be represented in the conceptual model. There are three key object categories:

- *People*—There are always people in any story about working and engaging with an interactive product. The people in the story could be only the user herself

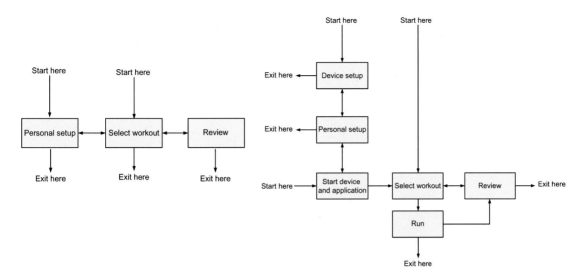

FIGURE 13.4:
An example of workflows for the running example. The left-hand diagram is for the desktop interaction channel, and the right-hand diagram is for the mobile interaction channel.

or himself or the user and any other people involved. In the running example, the object-type "people" include the runner herself and, in some cases, other runners.

- *Tangibles*—A very common object type is physical and tangible entities, that is, objects the user or users can see, touch, and manipulate physically. In the running example, the running sensors, such as HR sensor and monitor, the GPS receiver, a music player, or the road itself, are very tangible objects with which the runner interacts.

- *Abstract*—Finally, the third common object category includes abstract objects. It is very tempting to follow the philosophers and define abstract objects by what they are not: they are not people and not any tangible object.[1] Abstract objects could also be information items. In the running example, a workout plan or a workout that took place is an abstract object with which the user interacts. Such abstract objects include information about the workout activities.

In many cases, some or all types of objects are represented in the detailed design of the interactive product by data, that is, by a collection of parameters. For example, parameters making up a personal account represent the runner herself. Parameters describing the performance during a specific run represent the abstract object of a workout that took place.

You can conduct the object-action analysis based on the persona and scenarios. In its simplest form, you identify in the scenario all the objects and their associated actions. Considering the multichannel and cross channel design challenge, you should also indicate which objects and actions relate to which channel. Table 13.3 presents an example of such an analysis of the objects and actions in the running example.

---

[1]Lewis (1986), citing Frege's writings, suggested the way of negation as a way to define the abstract: "An object is abstract if and only if it is both non-mental and non-sensible."

TABLE 13.3:
Object-action analysis of the scenario in the running example

Scenario	Interaction channel	Objects	Actions (some implied from the scenario)
Jake loves running with a heart rate (HR) monitor, a running tracking program that plays music, and always has his phone with him	Mobile	Sensor (HR monitor) A mobile app Phone	Wear Use
Jake set up a personal account through the miCoach website on his desktop computer, which later linked and synchronized with the account on the mobile app	Mobile Desktop	Personal account	Configure Modify Search and select Activate
Jake could easily set up the sensors and the app to connect and work	Mobile	Sensors App	Configure Modify Search and select Activate
Jake prepared several workout plans that included defining parameters such as routes, distances, desired pace, and playlists	Mobile Desktop	Workout (planned)	Build Modify Search and select
Every time he prepared to run, he would select one of the workout plans and then start	Mobile	Workout (planned)	Build Modify Search and select
While running, he looks at his location and performance in terms of HR, distance, time, and speed by browsing the miCoach app	Mobile	Real-time workout	Activate View Delete Save
He would always review the full details of the recent run, compare them with previous runs	Mobile Desktop	Previous workouts	Review Delete Share

This is a partial analysis aimed at illustrating the analysis components.

Journey and experience map

Mapping user journey and experience is an effective way to integrate tasks and objects and represent their combined impact. Moreover, it is a very effective way for delineating the various channels in user and usage scenarios. It is highly useful in identifying user pain points to establish needs, prioritize features, and prioritize design and development efforts.

In its most fundamental form, journey mapping, borrowed from the service design discipline, is a matrix-based representation of user main phases and tasks through a full life cycle interaction with the product, along with interaction channels and touch points (interaction points with objects in the domain or subject matter). A journey map for the running example is presented in Figure 13.5.

Usability requirements

Learnability, effectiveness, efficiency, and satisfaction were introduced in the first part of the book as key elements of usability and user experience. In addition, the analysis of these elements suggested that the conceptual model could have an impact on them. Consequently, before you start developing the conceptual model, you should formulate

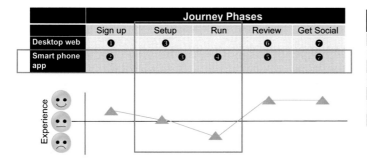

	Journey Phases						Touch point	Details
	Sign up	Setup	Run	Review	Get Social			
Desktop web	❶	❸		❻	❼		❶	Setting a personal account
Smart phone app	❷		❸ ❹	❺	❼		❷	Setting the personal account
							❸	Setting planned workouts and sensors
							❹	Viewing performance while running
							❺	Reviewing recent workouts
							❻	Reviewing and editing previous workouts
							❼	Sharing previous workout performance

FIGURE 13.5:
An example for a simple journey map for the running example. The part in the journey that is framed with the red rectangle highlights the phases with a poorer user experience according to the scenarios.

the usability and user experience requirements. The formulation of such requirements is an important outcome of user research.

What does it mean, practically, to have usability requirements? Remember, for example, there can be some trade-off between effectiveness and efficiency. You should determine whether the model should support effective interaction at the possible expense of less efficiency, or perhaps the opposite, and formulate it as a requirement. In addition to being an outcome of user research, determining usability requirements should be related to the strategic aspects of the product.

The strategic aspects

Let us go back to strategic understanding and thinking. We must be aware of business objectives and ensure those are met directly or indirectly through the conceptual model. These include understanding the motivation for developing the product and other business considerations such as partners, branding, and future plans. Another important strategic aspect is the way the design and development will be managed as a project.

User Research—Key Practical Points

- Do it! Have all team members and stakeholders involved.
- Clearly define your research questions.
- Consider data sources and collection techniques that will answer your research questions.
- Identify user profiles, develop personas, and for each construct usage scenarios.
- Perform task analysis and delineate workflows.
- Map objects and actions.
- Map user journey and experience.
- Formulate usability and experience requirements.
- Consider the wider business aspects.

Note that the consideration of the strategic aspects is included here as part of the prerequisite user research. In other words, some of the data you should gather and analyze should include the strategic aspects of the product and the project.

We are now ready to start the conceptual design and construct the conceptual model. As you will see, there is very little magic and mystery in the transition from the research to design. The following are several methodical steps that can bridge the perceived mystical gap between research and design.

Functional Chunks: Construct the Essential Foundation

In the first step of conceptual design, we define the functional chunks. This is the step where we put some order in the subject matter of the system. In the world of designing Web sites, this is equivalent to the first step of putting together the information architecture. In this step, we rely heavily on some of the user research and analyses we did. Analyses such as the task analysis and object-action mapping guide us in defining the functional chunks and the links between them.

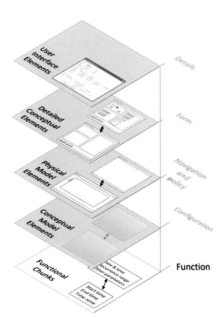

What's in This Step?

There are three activities when we start at the function level:

1. Define the functional chunks.
2. Link them.
3. Pause and check yourself.

DEFINE FUNCTIONAL CHUNKS

We start with functions. Based on the research we have done, functions are the various actions, elements, and parameters that together make up the subject matter of the product. The first activity in constructing the conceptual model is to group functions into chunks. What are the key drivers to define functional chunks? Let us consider here two:

A priori: Sometimes, there are *a priori* considerations for how to chunk the functions. These can be driven by business considerations and market trends, branding strategies, reflection of the underlying technology of the product, and a good representation of how users perceive the subject matter or, in other words, their mental model.

Emergent: The chunks emerge from an empirical discovery process (e.g., a focus group or open card sorting or employing the KJ method, from the task analysis, or based on the object-action analysis) with no *a priori* considerations.

Regardless of whether the criteria for chunking are *a priori* or emergent, we would like those chunks to be meaningful. What is a meaningful chunk? A real evasive definition of a meaningful chunk is whatever we define as meaningful according to certain criteria. But seriously, what should be the criteria for defining meaningful functional chunks? We can characterize meaningful functional chunks around two typical cores: tasks or objects. Let us start with defining simple functional chunks, that is, chunks with a single core. Later, we will get to defining complex chunks, which we will call compound chunks.

Task-oriented functional chunks

Definition: A user task is the core of a task-oriented functional chunk.

Appropriateness: Define task-oriented functional chunks when

- they fit users' mental models. The results of a task analysis validated by users can be viewed as reflecting users' mental models. See the functional chunks for the mobile and desktop channels in the running example in Figure 14.1,
- workflow is very task-oriented and structured. See the functional chunks for the mobile channel in the running example in Figure 14.2. No functional chunks are presented for the desktop channel since the workflow has only three steps, each distinct with respect to the tasks they represent (see Figure 13.4, the left-hand diagram).

The core of the task-oriented functional chunks in the running example, presented in Figures 14.1 and 14.2, are the tasks. The task-oriented functional chunks for the mobile channel (top of Figure 14.1) are as follows: device and personal setup, plan workout,

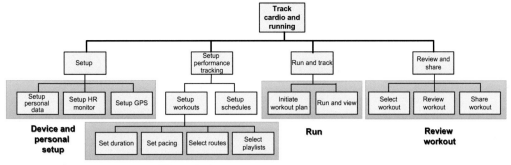

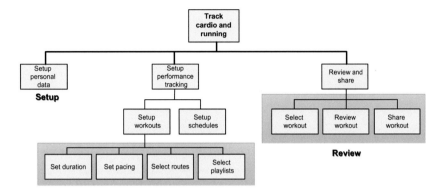

FIGURE 14.1:
Simple task-oriented functional chunks, denoted by the background rectangles, based on a hierarchical task analysis in the running example. The functional chunks for the mobile channel are at the top and for the desktop channel at the bottom.

FIGURE 14.2:
Simple task-oriented functional chunks, denoted by the background rectangles, based on task flow in the running example.

run, and review. The task-oriented functional chunks for the desktop channel (bottom of Figure 14.1) are as follows: setup, plan workout, and review. Similarly, the task-oriented functional chunks based on the workflow (Figure 14.2) are as follows: setup, run, and review. We later transform those into conceptual model elements.

Object-oriented functional chunks

Definition: The core of an object-oriented functional chunk is an object from the domain of the product. A clear distinction should be made between domain or subject matter objects and implementation objects. When looking for object-oriented functional chunks, those must reflect objects in the subject matter.

Appropriateness: Define object-oriented functional chunks when

- they fit users' mental models,
- workflow reflects object-oriented interactions.

The core of the object-oriented functional chunks in the running example, presented in Figure 14.3, is an object. The objects, for the mobile channel, are Workout, with planned, real-time, and previous workouts as instances of this object. Similarly, the objects, for the desktop channel, are Workout, presented in Figure 14.4, with planned and previous workouts as instances of that object.

FIGURE 14.3:
Object-oriented functional chunks for the mobile channel in the running example.

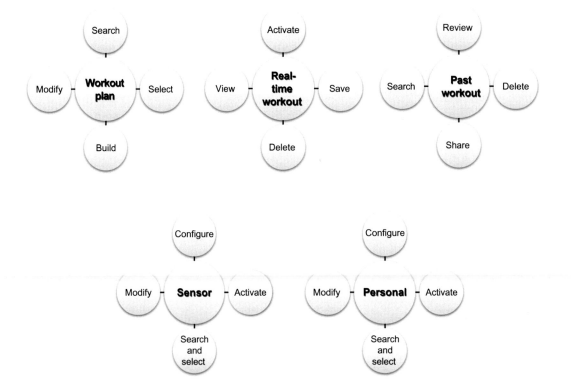

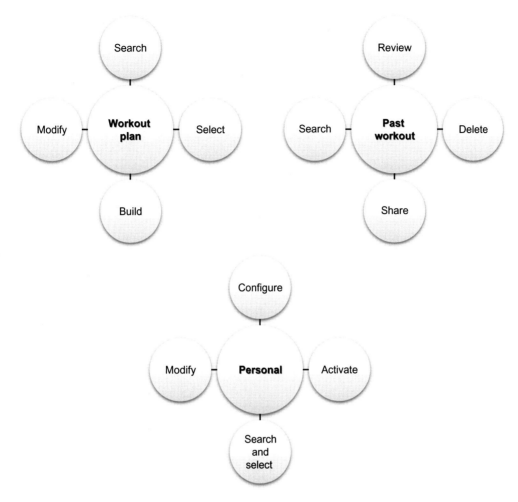

FIGURE 14.4:
Simple object-oriented functional chunks for the desktop channel in the running example.

LINK FUNCTIONAL CHUNKS

The next step after defining the functional chunks, be they task- or object-oriented, is to outline the links between the chunks. The links between functional chunks depend on task structure, interaction flow, and affinities between objects. Consider also the strength of the links. The links can be stronger if the chunks are used together frequently or if they are dependent upon each other in the interaction flow.

Link simple task-oriented chunks that

- serve the same goal, in a product with multiple goals;
- are part of the same task workflow;
- are sequential in a given task workflow;
- are performed frequently together.

For example, there are two setup-oriented simple functional chunks in Figure 14.2: (1) device and personal setup and (2) setting up a workout plan. Both can be further linked because they serve the same goal of setting up parameters in the system before running. In addition, both can be part of the same task flow, typically in a first-time use when the user will setup all aspects of the product. Finally, both can be sequential in that one would first set up the device and then proceed with the personal setup.

While defining those links, you may end up redefining some of the functional chunks. Specifically, you may consider several interlinked chunks as making up a *compound functional chunk*. In our running example, the two linked functional chunks device and personal setup and setting up workout plans can be redefined as a setup compound functional chunk, as can be seen at the top diagram of Figure 14.5, for the mobile channel. Similarly, setting up the personal account and the workout plans can be chunked into a setup compound functional chunk for the desktop channel, as is shown at the bottom of Figure 14.5.

We can employ a similar approach to the object-oriented chunks. Link simple object-oriented chunks that

- represent objects having a common meaning,
- represent objects that have some affinity between them.

FIGURE 14.5:
Redefining compound task-oriented functional chunks. The top diagram depicts the compound chunks for the mobile channel, and the bottom diagram is the compound functional chunks for the desktop channel.

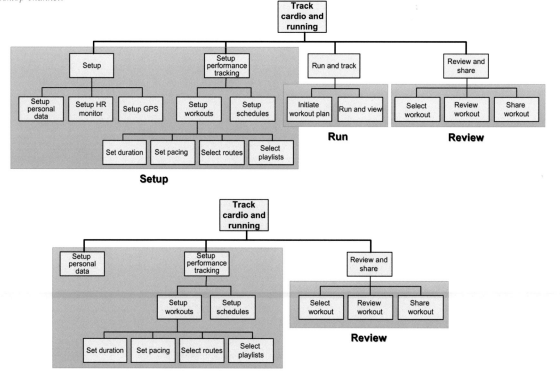

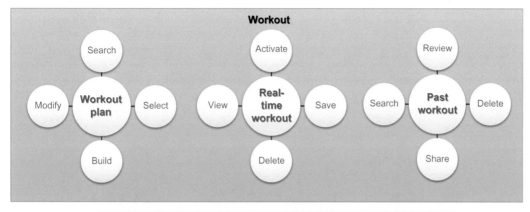

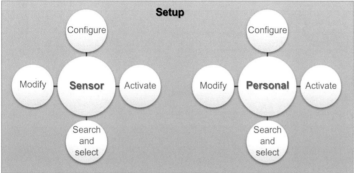

FIGURE 14.6:
*Compound object-
oriented functional chunks
in the running example for
the mobile channel.*

For example, in Figure 14.6, we can see two compound functional chunks for the mobile channel in the running example. The top compound functional chunk is "Workout" and it combines all the workout object-oriented simple chunks shown first in Figure 14.3. These are combined to a single compound functional chunk because all objects have common meaning for the user and can fit the mental model. Note in Figure 14.6 another compound functional chunk combining the personal account and sensor functional chunk. These two objects have some affinity between them: Both represent objects that are engaged before running. These two object-oriented functional chunks are combined into a task-oriented compound functional chunk and are in line with what we came up with when we examined the definition of task-oriented compound chunks. We can employ the same line of reasoning and define an object-oriented compound chunk for the desktop channel in the running example, as is presented in Figure 14.7.

In addition to all of the above criteria, you can also link simple task-oriented or object-oriented chunks as a function of

* usage context (when functional chunks are relevant to or are dealt with in the same usage context and are distinct from other functional chunks dealt with in other usage contexts),

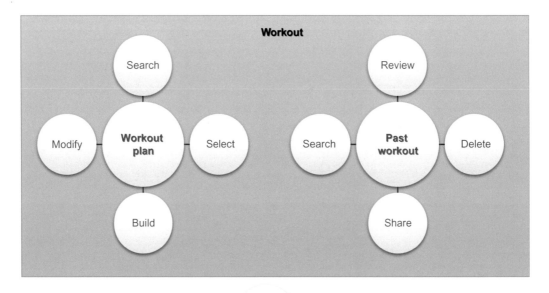

FIGURE 14.7:

*Compound object-
oriented functional chunks
in the running example for
the desktop channel.*

- interaction channel (when functional chunks are typically dealt with in a given interaction channel and are distinct from other functional chunks dealt with in other channels).

Following the workflow in the running example, we can distinguish between several usage contexts or states: initial setup, before running, during running, and after running. In the task analysis of the running example (Figure 14.1), the tasks associated with reviewing running performance can be performed only after running. The running functional chunks (real-time information during the run itself) could be done only on a mobile device such as a smartphone or a running wristwatch. In contrast, tasks associated with setting the personal account or reviewing running performance can be done in channels such as a desktop computer Web site or program and an app or Web site on a mobile device such as a tablet or a smartphone, but it cannot be done in a very limited fashion on a running wristwatch. These considerations should be taken into account when defining the compound functional chunks as either task-oriented or object-oriented or both.

The decisions on compound functional chunks will later influence the decision of how to assign conceptual elements to physical places. It is more reasonable to assign a compound functional chunk to a single physical place than have each of the simple functional chunks in a separate physical place. This in turn will influence navigation and navigation policy, as we will see soon.

CHECKPOINT: REVISIT AND REVISE

At this point, based on user research and analysis, you have defined simple and confound functional chunks and linked between them. As you realize, not all is resolved and you may be far from a conclusion. You may not be sure about the definitions of the chunks and/or the links between them. You may have several alternative definitions and links. You may not be ready to make a concluding decision about these.

The process should be iterative. It would be a good practice at this point to revisit what you have done. You may go back all the way to user research and consider collecting more data. You may go back and redo your task analysis or refine personas and scenarios or even add or remove personas and scenarios. You may consider going back to the stakeholders you work with and validating the chunking strategy with them.

The Running Experience Example: Revisiting Functional Chunks and Iterating

1. Collect more data on whether runners like to review their performance immediately after running or they can wait until they get to a tablet, a laptop, or a desktop computer.
2. Consider developing a new persona and scenarios for those who run and review performance together.
3. Redo task analysis and workflow mapping to consider combining running and review into a compound functional chunk.

PROJECT MANAGEMENT CONSIDERATIONS

We now have a definition of functional chunks. Looking at the broader context of product development projects, there is a strong tendency to define the minimum viable product (MVP), particularly with start-ups using lean and agile approaches. Our job is to ensure there will not be gaps in features essential to UX. In other words, let us consider the most viable experience (MVX). In this early stage, it is ensuring functional chunks are well defined in a way that users can understand; in other words, they can match existing mental models or contribute to developing a new one.

Functional Chunks—Key Practical Points

- Use the task analysis, workflow, and object-action analysis to define functional chunks that are either task-oriented or object-oriented. Remember, objects can be information items as well.
- Link between functional chunks to define compound chunks.
- Outcomes: diagrams with the functional chunks.
- Evaluate with team members and other stakeholders to validate the definitions.

Configuration: Draw Your First Rough Sketch of the Conceptual Model

We want to get fast to something we can show. Whereas putting together the functional chunks and the functional architecture is an essential step that we should share with all stakeholders, it is still hard for some to get a clear sense of how the user interface itself will evolve from it. In the configuration step, we sketch something that looks like a model and you can even illustrate, on an abstract level, how the user will interact with it. It is your first napkin sketch, as it were, the first visualization of the concept.

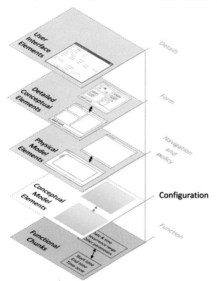

What's in This Step?

The configuration layer activities are the following:

1. Define and configure conceptual model elements.
2. Identify pivotal elements.
3. Reconfigure the model.
4. Checkpoint.

DEFINE AND CONFIGURE CONCEPTUAL MODEL ELEMENTS

Once you defined the functional chunks, be they simple or compound, you can now transform them into conceptual model elements. As was explained in the primer, a more abstract representation of the functional chunks supports the understanding, further development, and assessment of the conceptual model. There are two steps in configuring the conceptual model:

1. Represent each functional chunk as a conceptual model element. At this point, we may have simple task-oriented or object-oriented functional chunks. In addition, we have the desired interaction flow. Regardless of their type and simplicity, we should abstract the chunks that fit best the interaction flow. Thus, we may end up with conceptual model elements representing some of the task-oriented and/or some of the object-oriented. See the conceptual elements of the running example in Figure 15.1. Note that some of the elements represent objects such as workouts, and some represent tasks such as review and share.
2. Define compound conceptual elements, when relevant, based on links between the elements, which in turn are based on the links between the functional chunks. Note that at this point, the links do not convey all the details of the full navigation map. See Figure 15.2 with the mobile and the desktop interaction channels.

The resulting configuration is the foundation for the conceptual model.

LOOK FOR A PIVOTAL ELEMENT IN THE CONFIGURATION

The conceptual model should have a meaningful configuration. The mere linking of conceptual elements may not always convey a meaningful configuration. You should

FIGURE 15.1:
Conceptual model elements for the running example. Note that these elements are relevant to both desktop and mobile interaction channels.

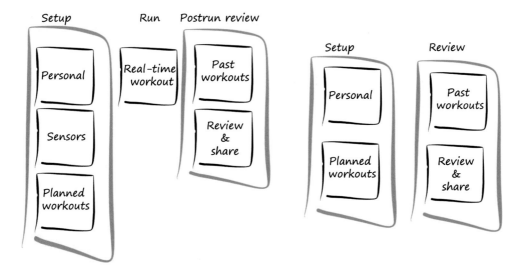

FIGURE 15.2:
Compound conceptual elements in the running example based on links between the simple functional chunks for the mobile interaction channel in the left-hand side and for the desktop channel in the right-hand side.

look at it and it should make sense to you. By itself, it should tell the story of the product. A meaningful configuration is one that represents well mental models or would easily induce a new mental model that can facilitate understanding, or workflow, or platform and context constraints or business and brand considerations. Looking for a meaningful configuration is an essential step in transforming a bunch of linked elements into a coherent conceptual model. The conceptual model typologies presented and discussed in the primer are the most common examples for such coherent models.

In order to assess the configuration and transform it into a meaningful one, ask yourself if there is a conceptual element or several tightly linked elements that can be considered as pivotal. As examples, pivotal concepts in the context of human experience with interactive systems are writing a document in a word processing program, preparing a slide in a show, sketching on a canvas in a drawing program, setting an appointment in a calendar application, writing and sending a tweet, or monitoring an automatic process.

Pivotal elements would be those meeting one or several of the following criteria:

- used very frequently,
- critical and essential,
- the most common steady state, and
- best represent the business objective and/or the brand.

Look for a pivotal element by revisiting the following:

- personas and scenarios,
- task analysis,
- key user interface and usability requirements,
- business objectives and brand considerations,
- usage context, and
- device/channel constraints.

In the running example, we can find two pivotal elements, based on the user research: the workout and, of course, running (Figure 15.3). The workout element seems to appear consistently in all workflows and tasks in both the mobile and desktop channels. The user engages with the workout element before, during, and after running. Another element that emerges as pivotal is anything that has to do with running: planning for it, engaging with it, and reviewing it later. The running element is particularly pivotal for the mobile channel that primarily serves that purpose.

It is important to emphasize that a pivotal conceptual element in the conceptual model does not have to be literally a central one. In examining the hub and spokes model discussed in the primer, that model has the hub literally in the center where most of the interaction takes place and after any other supplementary interaction, the user returns to that central place, the hub. In contrast, the single sequence or the network models do not seem to have a central hub as such. Nevertheless, such models do have a pivotal element. For example, in a web site having a network conceptual model, the home page can be that hub. In an installation wizard application with a single sequence

FIGURE 15.3:
Possibilities for pivotal elements in the running experience example.

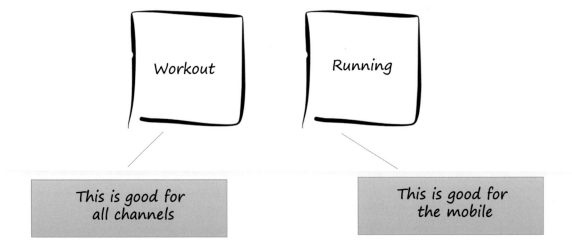

model, the starting place could be that pivotal point. In a hierarchy conceptual model, the root could be that pivotal element.

RECONFIGURE THE MODEL

It is now time to revisit the configuration of the conceptual elements in order to express the pivotal element you identified. It is not merely a graphic rotation or rearrangement. The objective is to have the reconfigured model in such a way that it will either fit better an existing mental model or be intuitively understood so it can help create a new mental model. In addition, the reconfiguration will facilitate the next step of outlining the navigation map.

In the running example, we chose the workout as the pivotal element for the reconfigured conceptual model. It is the choice since it appears in all workflows and tasks, in both channels, and in most states and phases of the user journey. The reconfigured conceptual models for the mobile and desktop channels are presented in Figures 15.4 and 15.5, respectively. Note that the conceptual models for both channels have several common compound elements: the workout, prerun setup, and postrun. It will support a more transparent user experience across the two channels. In addition, the conceptual model of the mobile channel has an additional element for the real-time workout.

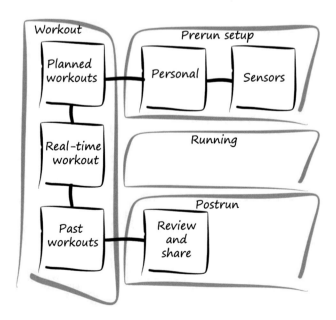

FIGURE 15.4:
Reconfigured conceptual model for the mobile channel in the running example.

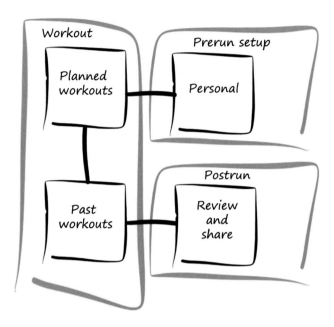

CHECKPOINT: REVISIT AND REVISE

The Running Experience Example: Revisiting Configuration and Iterating

1. Revisit user research data about frequency of use of the two candidate pivotal elements: the workout and real-time running.
2. Consider distinguishing clearly between the contexts and channels when planning or reviewing workouts in comparison with the real-time running.
3. Assess whether you have two conceptual models, one for real-time running with a mobile channel and one for the nonrunning context with other channels.

At this point, we have something that is a model: elements, representing functional chunks, and their interrelations. An important aspect to revisit now is the configuration, that is, the links representing relations. In particular, it is important to reassess the decision on the pivotal element if you have one. You should revisit the relevant aspects and parameters in the user research that you used to make that decision.

PROJECT MANAGEMENT CONSIDERATIONS

We now have a sketch, that is, we have our "architectural plan" for the user interface. Can we share it already? Assuming you work closely with stakeholders, users in particular, you should share it with them. Stakeholders should provide some preliminary feedback on this representation that will evolve into the detailed conceptual model and then transition into detailed design. What of the agile and lean approaches who want to implement something and deliver it fast? We can achieve it with a teamwork approach, and within that team, we should also be the gatekeepers. Our job is ensuring that such "architectural plan" exists and that users can understand it.

However, it is often hard to share abstract representations with everyone. Some members of the team and stakeholders may need to see something more concrete. They may want to see at least more detailed wire frames to get a better understanding of the fundamental concept. It is important to emphasize that there is nothing in the methodology outlined here to discourage you from taking some of the conceptual model elements and run ahead through the steps to provide more details. You can then get back to further develop the conceptual model or further develop the other elements. As was said earlier on, the goal is not necessarily to follow a linear process but rather ensure that all layers of the design are covered and well integrated at the end.

Configuration—Key Practical Points

- Use the functional chunks, simple or compound, to define conceptual model elements.
- The conceptual elements can be based on combinations of task- and object-oriented functional chunks.
- Configure the elements: delineate the links between the elements.
- Use user research and determine if there is a pivotal element—one that is the most important or most frequently used.
- Reconfigure the model.
- The outcome is a diagram representing the conceptual elements and their configuration.
- Evaluate with team members and other stakeholders to validate the model.

Navigation Map: Moving from One Place to Another

16

The main aspect of the navigation and policy layer is the navigation map of the conceptual model. As discussed in the primer part of the book, getting to the full navigation map is more than just having the routes between conceptual elements. The full map includes also the navigation policy (modality) based on the assignment of conceptual elements to physical places. However, here in the step-by-step methodology, we will divide this layer into two steps: we outline the navigation map, explained in this chapter, and then in the next chapter, we will cover the physical assignment and finalize the navigation policy.

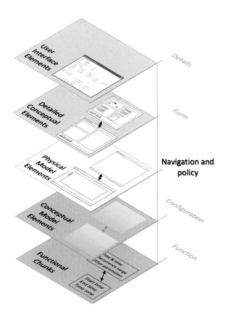

What's in This Step?

The activities in the navigation and policy layer are the following:

1. Outline navigation map.
2. Evaluate and revise.

OUTLINE NAVIGATION MAP

Having determined a pivotal conceptual element, and having reconfigured the model to accommodate that element, brings us to the navigation map. As we progress with the design process, we will later refine the navigation map by considering the assignment of conceptual elements to physical places and determining the navigation policy. Nevertheless, for now, we outline the conceptual navigation map by defining the following:

- Entry and exit conceptual elements
- The navigation directionality of the links between the conceptual elements

In order to determine these, you should use the reconfigured model based on the identified pivotal element and the interaction workflow. With respect to navigation, the concept of a pivotal element is such that we want to have the user get to it as soon as possible. It could either be the starting point or have the shortest route to it. This should not only correspond to the typical interaction workflow but also support all other possible workflows that can be uncovered through user research or defined based on user research.

The navigation maps for the mobile and desktop channels in our running example are presented in Figures 16.1 and 16.2, respectively. Note that in both of them, we have several entry and exit places. We will need to consider this when we assign the elements to physical places and fine-tune the navigation map.

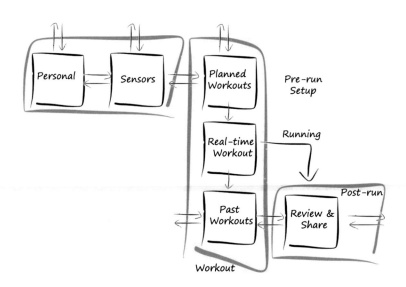

FIGURE 16.1:
Conceptual navigation map for the mobile channel in the running example.

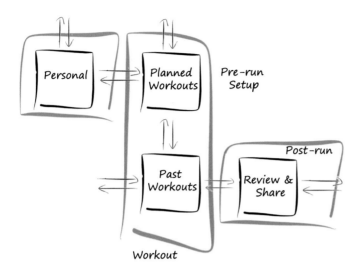

FIGURE 16.2:
Conceptual navigation map for the desktop channel in the running example.

The navigation maps preserve all the conceptual elements of the model, but we can rearrange the sketch in a way that reflects the journey map and workflow. In the examples in Figures 16.1 and 16.2, the elements are arranged in a way that the most typical and common workflows progress from left to right and from top to bottom. Typical workflow, with either the mobile or the desktop channels, starts with the prerun setup, then progresses to the running itself, and concludes with the postrun activities. The two-way arrows that break through the boxes depicting the compound elements represent start and exit places of the interactions. Note that the pivotal status of the workout is consistent in both navigation maps.

EVALUATE AND REVISE

What we have in our hands at this point is a conceptual model including the navigation map. Is it a valid model? Is it a good model? In other words, is this model appropriate to user needs or does it support business objectives? It could be rather challenging to address such questions when all we really have is a sketched diagram. Nevertheless, we can address some fundamental questions in assessing the validity and goodness of the model.

First, who should be involved in the evaluation? Ideally, representatives of all stakeholders should be involved. Those include users, the design and development team, and representatives of the business aspects of the product. Second, since at this point all we have are sketches, we can run an inspection-style evaluation of the model.

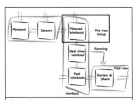

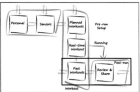

The first time Jake used the application, he started with the Setup screen. He first set his account and then went on to configure the HR monitor to work with the application while he runs. As part of his planning he went on to define several planned workouts.	From the Setup screen he navigated to the Planned Workouts screen. He setup several workouts according to varying distances he was planning to run at different times.	When he ran, he would glance at the screen of his smart phone, and could see some interesting parameters of his running performance, in addition to a map showing where he was.	Once he completed his run, the application switched to a screen summarizing his most recent run where could view numeric parameters and graphs summarizing his performance. He could also access summaries of previous runs.

FIGURE 16.3:

An evaluation scenario along with the relevant portion of the conceptual model for each step in the scenario (highlighted with the black frame).

This inspection should involve a scenario walkthrough through the conceptual model (Figure 16.3) with some think-alouds.

To aid such an inspection, here is a checklist based on three dimensions:

The conceptual model—Use the following list of questions to evaluate the validity and goodness of the model by the following:

- Does it represent all functional chunks?
- Does it express all the relevant links between the elements, reflecting links between chunks?
- Does the navigation map support the workflow?
- Is the model's complexity level appropriate to user profiles and task structuredness?

Human performance—The implications of the conceptual model for human performance and usability are assessed with the following questions:

- Does the model support location awareness?
- Will the model support visual search?
- Will the model decrease operational load?
- Does the model reduce memory load?

Usability and user experience—Assessing the utilitarian aspect of the concept along with some speculation on user experience aspects with the following questions:

- Will the model support learnability?
- Will the model support effective interaction?
- Will the model support efficiency?
- Will the model support positive experience?

Table 16.1 presents an example of using this checklist in the evaluation of the conceptual model presented in Figure 16.2.

Evaluation dimension	Assessment			Comments
	Fully	**Partially**	**Not at all**	
The conceptual model				
Does it represent all functional chunks?		✓		Some new possible functions came up during the evaluation. See further comments below
Does it express all the relevant links between the elements, reflecting links between chunks?		✓		Need to consider the possibility of linking between real-time workout directly to the review and share, particularly share in real-time
Does the navigation map support the workflow?		✓		Need to assess whether setting a default workout plan and start interaction directly from that point
Is the model's complexity level appropriate to user profiles and task structuredness?	✓			The model seems simple and straightforward
Human performance				
Does the model support location awareness?	✓			
Will the model support effective visual search?	✓			It seems according to the number of conceptual elements that effective visual search is supported
Will the model decrease operational load?		✓		The lack of direct link to real-time workout as a default starting point may result in some operational load
Does the model reduce memory load?	✓			
Usability and user experience				
Will the model support learnability?	✓			
Will the model support effective interaction?	✓			
Will the model support efficiency?		✓		See comment above regarding possible operational load
Will the model support positive experience?	✓			

TABLE 16.1:
An inspection-style evaluation of the conceptual model of the mobile channel in the running experience example

PROJECT MANAGEMENT CONSIDERATIONS

At this point, we have a conceptual model with the navigation map. Having conducted an evaluation and, when relevant, done some revisions, we can say we have a validated model. What is the impact of this step and its outcome?

We should consider several points with respect to what we can do with this outcome. Remember, this is an interim outcome. We are still in the process and this is work in progress. By analogy, if we view the process as building a house, we have just laid the foundation. The significance and impact of this foundational model are the following:

1. We have a conceptual model founded on user research, rigorous methodology, and scientific underpinnings.
2. We have a conceptual model that has undergone a formative evaluation.
3. We have a detailed sketch of the conceptual model we can share with stakeholders.
4. We have a well-defined framework with which we can proceed towards the detailed design.
5. We have a well-defined framework within which we can start prototyping some parts of the product.

As we indicated in the previous step, the outcome here may not be concrete enough for some team members and stakeholders to relate to. You can run ahead through the next steps for some of the elements in order to provide a more concrete illustration of the model. But always make sure that at the end, you do not skip the steps suggested to ensure a coherent conceptual model.

Navigation Map—Key Practical Points

- Outline the navigation map based on scenarios and workflows.
- Include in the navigation map entry points, exit points, and routes that can be taken through the conceptual model.
- Overlay the conceptual model diagram with arrows indicating all navigational information.
- Validate the model and the navigation map by preparing a scenario with the model to evaluate with team members and other stakeholders.

Navigation Policy: Define the "Rules of the Road"

17

As promised in the previous chapter, we continue here to fine-tune the navigation map by determining the physical assignment and finalizing the navigation policy. In terms of the layered framework, we are still on the navigation and policy layer. The outcome of this step is the detailed and fine-tuned navigation map with all the behaviors defined.

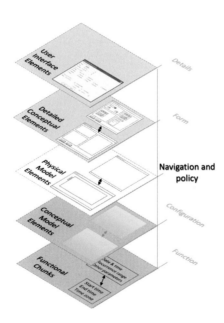

> ## What's in This Step?
>
> The relevant activities in navigation and policy for fine-tuning the navigation map are the following:
>
> 1. Define the physical place assignment.
> 2. Start prototyping.
> 3. Define policy (modality).
> 4. Revisit and revise.
> 5. Define operational principles.
> 6. Evaluate and revise.

DEFINE PHYSICAL PLACES FOR CONCEPTUAL ELEMENTS

While still far from making detailed implementation decisions, at this point, we should assign conceptual elements to their physical places. As explained in the primer part of this book, the assignment to physical places has an impact on navigation and interaction policy. You can use several decision criteria to assign conceptual elements to physical places as described below.

Human performance goals

The following human performance criteria have been outlined and discussed in the primer and can be considered as performance goals:

- Mental models and understanding
- Location awareness
- Visual search effectiveness
- Operational (executing actions) load
- Working memory load

We can use these performance goals as primary decision criteria for physical assignments (Table 17.1).

As always with human behavior, we may face trade-offs between goals. The very common one is the trade-off between increasing visual search effectiveness and reducing operational load. Resolve the trade-offs between the performance goals with additional implications from the user research analyses, context of use, and interaction channels.

Human performance goals	Conceptual	Physical assignment
Facilitate intuitive understanding	Express affinities between elements	All elements in one or few screens or windows Separate physical place for each chunk but all in one window or place (e.g., use a matrix model or use tabs within the same window)
Support location awareness	Keep elements in fewer places Shorten navigation routes required to complete tasks	
Minimize working memory load		
Reduce operational load		
Increase visual search effectiveness	Minimize number of functional elements in a single functional chunk	Have elements in several physical places to minimize the amount of details in a given physical place

TABLE 17.1:
Using human performance goals as criteria to determine physical assignment of conceptual models

Analyses implications

The analyses relevant to assigning conceptual model elements to physical locations are task analysis, object-action analysis, and the desired interaction flow. These analyses have the following outcomes and implications:

How often do we do something?—One of the outcomes of task analysis is the frequency with which tasks are performed or are expected to be performed. Tasks and their associated conceptual elements with similar frequencies can be considered for the same physical place or in close proximity.

What do we do at the same time?—An outcome of all the analyses is whether tasks and actions are typically performed at the same time or close to each other in time. Tasks and actions done at the same time, whether on the same object or different objects, can be considered for the same physical place or in close proximity.

What do we do one after another?—An outcome of the desired interaction flow and of the task analysis is the sequence with which tasks and actions are performed or supposed to be performed. Taken together with similar frequency and/or doing things at the same time, operations in a sequence can be considered for the same physical place or in close proximity.

What depends on what?—A primary outcome of the desired interaction flow, and also implied from the task analysis and object-action analysis, is the dependency between actions. Dependency is the requirement that a given action must precede another action. A simple, almost everyday example for dependency in so many programs and applications is between copy or cut and paste. Actions with dependency relations between them can be considered for the same physical place or in close proximity.

What do we see at the same time?—An outcome of all analyses is the required or expected visibility of tasks and objects. The visibility of a task or an object is the level with which the user is aware of their status. The analyst should identify those tasks or objects whose status should be visible to the user when interacting with other objects or performing another task. Tasks or objects requiring a similar level of visibility or tasks or object requiring visibility while engaged with other tasks or objects can be considered for the same physical place or in close proximity.

Intuitiveness and findability—An outcome of all analyses is the grouping of elements in a way that can facilitate intuitive understanding of the affinities among them and subsequently the ease with which to find what the user looks for. To increase intuitiveness and findability, tasks and objects with high affinity can be considered for the same physical place or in close proximity.

These analyses and their implications to physical assignment of conceptual model elements are summarized in the following table (Table 17.2).

TABLE 17.2:
Implications of several user research analyses on the physical assignment decisions

Analysis	Conceptual	Implications	Physical assignment
Task analysis	Task-oriented affinities	Similar frequency, likely sequence, likely concurrency	All elements in one or few screens or windows Separate physical place for each chunk but all in one window or place (e.g., use a matrix model or use tabs within the same window)
Object-action analysis	Object-oriented affinities	Likely concurrency, findability	
Desired interaction flow	Work flow	Sequence, dependency	

Context of usage, states, and modes

The context within which the user interacts with the system/product has an influence on the interaction. There are various levels to the context of use:

1. The physical context such as indoors vs. outdoors, stationary vs. mobile, day vs. night, or adequate vs. poor lighting conditions, quiet vs. noisy place, temperature and climate, and presence or absence of movement and vibrations.
2. The work flow context such as being in any given phase, step, state, or a mode. A common example is the distinction between an initial installation, setup, or configuration state, and the subsequent actual usage state.
3. The personal context, which consists of the state the user is in, such as a novice vs. experienced, wakeful vs. fatigued, highly motivated vs. burnt-out, and other states.
4. The social context, which refers to whether the user is alone or engages with the product with others. The presence of others could be group or teamwork, collaborative and sharing interaction, colocated or remote and distributed, and on a broader social context such as national, cultural, ethnic, or international associations and societies.

The analyst and designer should consider the combined implications of the various contextual factors on the assignment of conceptual elements to physical places. Having conceptual elements in the same physical place or in close proximity can support and facilitate interaction in the more challenging contexts, which are the ones that may include increased cognitive, or emotional, or physical workload on the user.

The interaction channels

The interaction channel is a very influential consideration when assigning conceptual elements to physical places. Interaction channel characteristics include stationary vs. mobile, screen size, interaction devices (e.g., keyboard and mouse, touch, buttons, gestures and movements, voice, gaze, and others), native style of look and feel, and the associated context of the channel (e.g., performing a financial transaction through an automated banking machine or through the bank's website or through a dedicated application on a small screen is typically associated with different contexts).

Of the various channel characteristics, screen size and the native style of look and feel tend to be the most influential factors on the decision of physical assignment of conceptual elements. Simply put, a small screen size introduces a serious obstacle to assigning several conceptual elements to a single physical place. The small screen size may either result in a considerable amount of scrolling and panning to reach all elements within the single physical place, or the size of elements will be decreased to fit better the small screen making them less legible.

Nevertheless, assigning conceptual elements to a single or few physical places can still be associated with a small-screen interaction channel. For example, a website originally designed for a large-screen desktop interaction channel can be adapted to the small screen via responsive design techniques. The resulting design ensures that the elements are not too small and support effective viewing, but they are still different places on a single web page, which requires scrolling and panning. Such an approach has the obvious benefits of not having to redesign the web site to small-screen channels, and a similar conceptual and detailed design can be implemented across channels.

The characteristics of the interaction channel can sometimes overturn decisions made based on performance goals, consideration of analyses outcomes, and contextual factors. In other words, a design decision to assign several elements to a single physical place may be overturned if the intended interaction channel has a small screen. This may also be associated with typical contextual factors for using small-screen devices such as mobility, being outdoors, experiencing varying environmental factors such as lighting and stability, and being in personal and social contexts that introduce more distractions and interruptions.

Business and brand considerations

Last, but definitely not the least, is the consideration of business objectives and implications of branding. A plausible requirement can be to include elements expressing the product brand, upselling, or cross selling (depending upon business partners). Including such elements requires their assignment to physical places, which in turn can impact the physical assignment of all other conceptual elements.

START PROTOTYPING

When assigning conceptual elements to physical places, we transition from representing the model in boxes and arrows to representing the model in terms of user interface elements. This is a good time to start prototyping. The idea is that the prototype you start constructing now will evolve and unfold as we proceed to add details to the conceptual model and transition later to the detailed design. The prototype will serve as a design tool, a communication channel with all stakeholders, and a tool for evaluation and testing. See an example for the initial prototyping of the conceptual model in the running example in Figure 17.1.

What we see in Figure 17.1 is the physical assignment of the conceptual elements in the model for each of the interaction channels in the running example, along with the abstract sketch of the model. In the top part of the figure, we see the conceptual model for the desktop channel, where all the elements were assigned to a single physical place, a web page. That place has two primary subplaces, two tabs, one for all the elements associated with the setup tasks and the other for all the elements that are some instances of a workout. Analyses implications and context of usage were used as criteria for such an assignment. More specifically, the setup tasks and the workout-related tasks are not done with the same frequency; they do not require concurrent or sequential operation and do not need to be visible at the same time. In addition, setup tasks are typically done before starting to run altogether, while interaction with the workout elements is done typically before and after every run. Recall that the navigation map allows for several entry and exit points. The physical assignment to a single web page nevertheless supports access to those several points.

In the bottom part of Figure 17.2, we see the conceptual model for the mobile channel, where all the elements were assigned to different screens (but remember that things are sometimes not what they seem, and more will be revealed in the next sections where we talk about policy and operational principles). Here, we used similar criteria to the ones we used for the desktop channel when assigning conceptual elements to physical places. Setup tasks are typically done before running altogether, with the addition of sensor setups that are done before running. Those were assigned to one screen. Each of the running elements was assigned to another screen since each is interacted with at different times and contexts during the running journey and each of those was assigned to a different screen. Recall that we have several entry and exit points in the navigation map. Due to the small-screen interaction channel, we cannot provide access to all of those points in the same manner we did for the desktop, the large-screen channel. Consequently, we need to "create" a new place that will serve as the main entry point and the access routes to all other elements. The top element in Figure 17.2 is that main entry point.

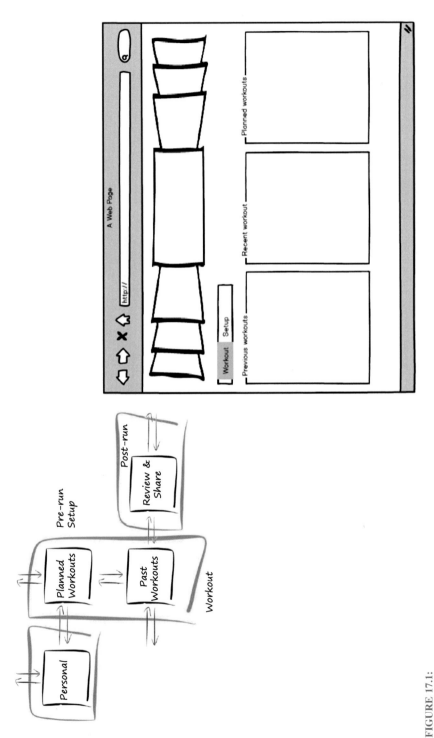

FIGURE 17.1:

Physical place assignment to conceptual elements in the running experience example for the conceptual model of the desktop channel. Built with Balsamiq at http://balsamiq. com/

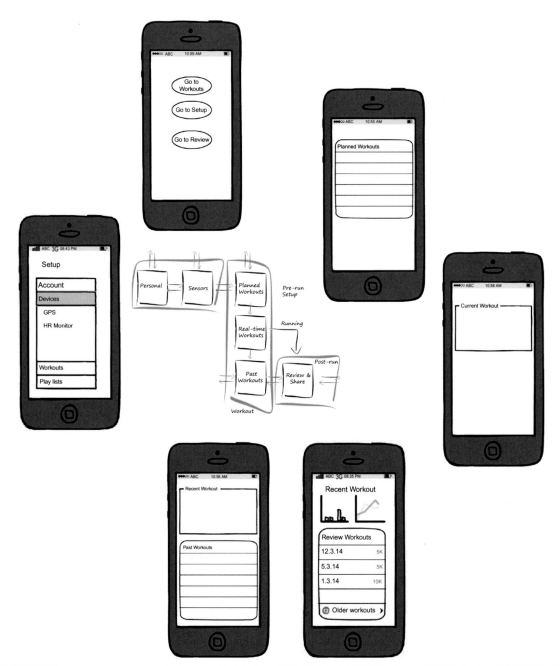

FIGURE 17.2:
Physical place assignment to conceptual elements in the running experience example for the conceptual model for the mobile (small screen) channel. Built with Balsamiq at http://balsamiq.com/

DEFINE POLICY

The navigation policy is an important issue you should address during the conceptual design phase, and it goes hand in hand with outlining the navigation map and assigning conceptual elements to physical places. Here is a reminder of what the navigation policy is. The policy deals fundamentally with the challenge of modality: While interacting with a given conceptual element in a given physical place, can the user also interact with another conceptual element in the same or different physical place? In making our decisions about the navigation and interaction policies, we follow the same criteria we use for determining the assignment of conceptual elements to physical places.

You make a large portion of the modality decisions while assigning conceptual elements to physical places (for a schematic example, go back to Table 6.1 in the primer part of this book). To determine the policy possibilities, do the following:

Fine-tune the analyses implications: Revisit the outcomes of the various analyses and verify the affinities between conceptual elements. Elements that we interact with or see at the same time should be independent. In other words, there is no modality between them regardless of whether they are assigned to the same or different physical place.

Follow channel-specific look and feel guidelines and conventions: Applying a modal vs. modeless policy in a large-screen interaction channel requires the definition of windows, dialogs, and screens as either modal or modeless relative to each other. However, in a small-screen channel, we can often end up with seemingly mutually exclusive elements only because they cannot be displayed and accessed at the same time due to screen size and not due to an intentional design decision.

Following the initial decisions on the physical assignment of conceptual elements in our running example, we move on to examine the resulting navigation policy. The details of the navigation policy for the example are in Table 17.3. We can see that with respect to modality, there is the same policy for both channels, even though both have a different physical assignment for the conceptual elements. Using the criteria for the physical place assignment, we see that for the desktop channel, the places for the setup tasks and the workout elements are mutually exclusive, even though they are all in the same place. The same modality applies for the mobile channel: The places for the different conceptual elements are mutually exclusive, but they are assigned to different physical places.

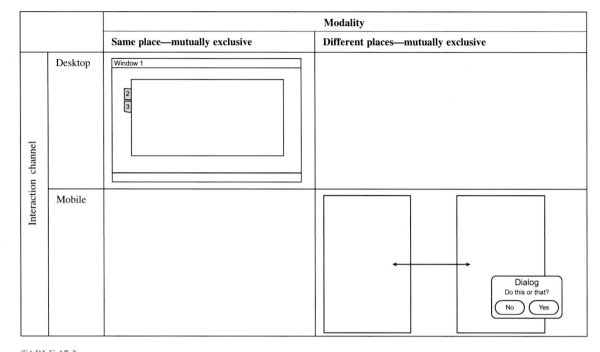

		Modality	
		Same place—mutually exclusive	**Different places—mutually exclusive**
Interaction channel	Desktop	Window 1 [2] [3]	
	Mobile		Dialog Do this or that? No Yes

TABLE 17.3:
The navigation policies for each of the channels in the running example

CHECKPOINT: REVISIT AND REVISE

At this point, we have a full conceptual model that consists of all the conceptual elements and interrelations, all assigned to physical places, and a navigation map and policy. We also have the model in the shape of an initial prototype. This is a good point to pause for another checkpoint and assess what we have.

The Running Experience Example: Revisiting the Navigation Map and Policy

1. Collect more data on the frequency of making setup and personal account changes. In addition, collect data on runners' familiarity with using a mobile device and how they use it before, during, and after running.
2. Consider changing the physical assignment and policy for the channels, in particular the mobile one due to the constraining conditions of usage (e.g., outdoors, weather and light conditions, and tiredness).
3. Revisit the need for an additional screen as a main entry point, and consider one of the other elements as a default entry place that will provide access to all other elements.

MORE IMPLICATIONS OF THE INTERACTION CHANNEL: THE OPERATIONAL PRINCIPLES

We have paid much attention to the characteristics of the interaction channel so far. Some of the physical assignment decisions were based on those characteristics and, in turn, influenced the navigation map and policy. It is time to ask whether the physical way the user interacts with the channel can also influence our design decisions regarding the conceptual model. Recall that we refer to this as the operational principles of the interaction. Refer to Table 6.2 in the first part of the book for a refresher on operational principles.

To consider the operational principles of the interaction channel, follow these steps:

- Identify and understand the channel's operational principles (i.e., characteristics of the physical interaction).
- Consider which of the operational principles are relevant given user research findings by asking the following questions:
  - Does it fit the persona?
  - Does it fit the context of usage?
  - Does it fit the frequency of use?
- Determine the influence of the relevant operational principles on physical assignment of conceptual elements and the navigation map and policy.
- Weigh benefits and costs.
- Consider revising the conceptual design (elements and navigation map).

Let us get back to our running example and see how considering the operational principles of the mobile interaction channel influences the conceptual design. See the following table for the considerations (Table 17.4).

Considerations	Details
Channel's operational principles	Touch-based swipe gesture to navigate to other places
Relevancy (based on user research)	Persona: familiar with the gesture and capable of performing it effectively Context: gestures can be done in most contexts Frequency: navigating between places is not done too often
Influence on the conceptual model	It may change the physical assignment of conceptual elements into a single place (in contrast to their previous assignment to different places)
Benefits	• Discarding with modal places • No need for on-screen navigation buttons
Costs	• May be problematic in some usage contexts such as while running, but this is rare

TABLE 17.4:
Considering the operational principles of the mobile channel in the running example

The last step is considering revision since the considerations suggest we should implement the swipe interaction in the mobile channel. You may recall that in the conceptual model we have so far, elements were assigned to different screens due to the small-screen constraints, thus making them mutually exclusive. By using the up-down swipe gesture to navigate, we can now assign several elements into the same physical place and swipe to navigate. Considering the workflow we uncovered and defined as part of our user research, a frequent transition is done between the "recent

FIGURE 17.3:
Implementing the swipe up and down operational principle in the mobile channel in the running example. Note that using this principle changes the conceptual model.

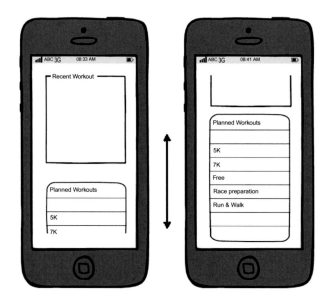

workout" and "planned workout" conceptual elements. Thus, we have assigned both of these into the same place. You can see the revised part of the conceptual model in Figure 17.3.

Having assigned several conceptual elements to the same physical place and taken advantage of the swipe operational principle allow us to revisit the necessity of a main entry point as a separate place, in the case of the mobile channel in the running example. Going back to user research and considering the dominance of the workout element in the findings, we can decide that the physical place for the combined elements of recent and planned workouts can become the default entry place, with access to other places.

EVALUATE AND REVISE

So far, we have assigned the conceptual elements to physical places, elaborated on the navigation map by adding the navigation policy, and implemented relevant operational principles. At this point, we should have evaluated again the validity and goodness of the unfolding conceptual model. One approach is to use the same list of questions we used before and with an inspection-style method focus on the same three dimensions: the conceptual model, human performance, and usability and user experience (see Table 17.5). Since we have a preliminary prototype or mock-up of the model, we can consider additional approaches to assessing the validity and goodness of the model. The key aspect of other approaches would be the incorporation of users in evaluation, in addition to expert inspections. The prototype can support an evaluation

Evaluation dimension	Assessment			Comments
	Fully	**Partially**	**Not at all**	
The conceptual model				
Does it represent all functional chunks?	✓			
Does it express all the relevant links between the elements, reflecting links between chunks?	✓			
Does the navigation map support the workflow?	✓			
Is the model's complexity level appropriate to user profiles and task structuredness?		✓		The combination of several elements to the same physical place, yet they are not visible immediately, may be confusing to some
Human performance				
Does the model support location awareness?		✓		The combination of several elements to the same physical place, yet they are not visible immediately, may be confusing to some
Will the model support effective visual search?	✓			It seems according to the number of conceptual elements that effective visual search will be supported
Will the model decrease operational load?	✓			
Does the model reduce memory load?		✓		The combination of several elements to the same physical place, yet they are not visible immediately, may be confusing to some
Usability and user experience				
Will the model support learnability?	✓			
Will the model support effective interaction?	✓			
Will the model support efficiency?	✓			
Will the model support positive experience?	✓			

TABLE 17.5:
An inspection-style evaluation of the advanced conceptual model in the running experience example

based on a walk-through of the participant following a scenario and walking through the model. As for metrics, we can use the questions in Table 17.5, or a think-aloud protocol, or even a standard summary usability and experience questionnaire (e.g., the SUS).

PROJECT MANAGEMENT CONSIDERATIONS

Very often, in many project contexts, this is the state we want to get to as soon as we can. This is because at this step, we have our ideas and the concept expressed in concrete terms that we can show and test. Does it feel like it took too long to get here? First, recall that we suggested earlier on that at various times in the process, you can "fast-forward" from the abstract state of some functional chunks and conceptual elements to a more concrete visualization and then get back to proceed with other elements.

Second, the project team can manage the process described so far effectively and efficiently. With respect to effectiveness, members of the project team and other stakeholders should be involved. This ensures that all perspectives, on all levels of the product from the very strategic to the very specific, are considered. It is effective because it can mitigate too-late realizations that some important considerations were missed or not appropriately addressed. With respect to efficiency, this process can be managed fast. While it may, at a first glance, seem like a long and multistep process, the duration and throughput depend on the scope and complexity of the domain and feature set. Let us take the running example and review the activities in getting to this point with hypothetical, yet quite realistic, time estimates for a quick process (Table 17.6).

TABLE 17.6:
Estimated project time for the running example

Activity	Participants	Time estimate
User research	Users, other stakeholders	2 days (including interviews and focus groups)
Generating functions and requirements from data	Project team	1 day
Chunking functions	Project team, stakeholders	0.5-day workshop with stakeholders
Model elements and configuration	Project team	0.5 day
Adding navigation and policy while prototyping	Project team	1 day
Formative evaluation and revision	Project team, stakeholders	1 day
Total for "Sketching the conceptual model"		6 days

Multichannel or cross channel interaction considerations: The most common challenge of many design and development projects is to ensure a consistent user experience across different interaction channels. Note that in the running example, we have addressed this challenge as well. While the approach in this example is to deal with the cross channel conceptual design in parallel, it is by no means a recommendation. As was said earlier in this part of the book, the approaches to dealing with multichannel and cross channel design are variable and may depend on a variety of factors and considerations that are out of the scope of this book. However, what we show here is that we can develop a cross channel conceptual model.

Navigation Policy—Key Practical Points

- Based on human performance goals, user research, and the interaction channel considerations, assign each conceptual element to a physical place.
- Define the navigation policy, which should include rules regarding modality of elements and how it influences navigation.
- Start prototyping the model with your favorite prototyping tool.
- Pause and revisit the model with focus on navigation and policy.
- Define how the user will interact physically with the model based on the operational principles of the interaction channel.
- Outcome: A preliminary prototype—with little details—of the conceptual model with the navigation map and policy.
- Evaluate with team members and other stakeholders to validate the model and the navigation map.

Form: Transition to Detailed Design

We reached the phase where we make the transition from the conceptual design to the detailed design. In terms of the layered framework, we are now at the form layer. Simply put, this is the time where our concept takes on a shape with details.

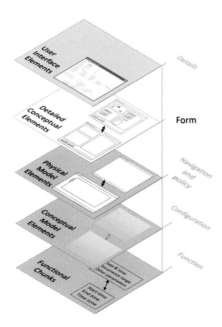

What's In This Step?

The relevant activities in the form layer are the following:

1. Consider having a metaphor.
2. Add details.
3. Develop a full storyboard.
4. Test and revise.

THE APPEARANCE CONCEPT: CONSIDER A METAPHOR

In the primer part of the book, we stated that if the user does not understand it, the user would not be able to use it. What is then a good way to facilitate the understanding of the conceptual model? Here, we need to consider if the conceptual model was developed to match an existing mental model of users, or if there is a need to help the user develop a new mental model to understand the conceptual model and be able to use the system. One common way in the world of UI and UX design to achieve this is to use metaphors. A metaphor is the representation of a concept in terms of another concept. Using something familiar as a metaphor can help users interact with elements that are otherwise too abstract or too technical to understand.

For example, the most famous, popular, and longest surviving metaphor in the world of human-computer interaction is "the desktop." Introduced first through the Xerox Star graphical user interface, the desktop metaphor represented computer and software elements in the familiar desktop environment with terminology and icons such as folders and files, the trashcan, and peripheral devices such as the printer. The "book" metaphor is another great example for combining an operational principle with a visual metaphor. E-readers or book reading applications on various devices typically have the application appear as a book with a hint of the book cover in the background and the look of pages about the binding midline. Moreover, the use of the book metaphor utilizes the touch-based interaction style of swiping from right to left to imitate the page flipping action we do to change pages with a real book (Figure 18.1).

Another aspect of the appearance concept is the assignment of conceptual elements to physical places. Once we do that, we get closer to considering the style with which the UI will appear. For example, deciding on tabs as the physical places for

On Mapping, Analogies, and Metaphors

When learning to use artifacts in our environment, and the same goes for interactive products, Norman (1999) talked about the principle of natural mapping. The principle refers to our ability to understand and know what to do or how to use something by mapping a correspondence between controls (e.g., buttons) and the elements we are trying to control or manipulate (e.g., an on-screen element).

Mapping is inherent in our ability to understand and solve problems by the use of analogies. Specifically, we can solve a problem by solving another problem that is analogous to the source problem. To do that, we first notice a correspondence the analogy between the two problems and then map the corresponding parts between the two problems. Based on the mapped correspondence, we can apply the solution from the analogous problem to the original problem (Catrambone & Holyoak, 1989; Gick & Holyoak, 1980, 1983; Holyoak & Thagard, 1995).

The use of metaphors is very similar to analogous reasoning. A metaphor helps us understand one concept or idea in terms of another (e.g., Lakkof & Johnson, 1980). In other words, we can map the correspondence between the metaphor and what we know or can understand.

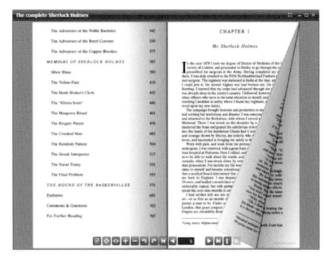

FIGURE 18.1:
A visual metaphor of a book combined with an operational principle of touch-based swiping gesture in e-readers.

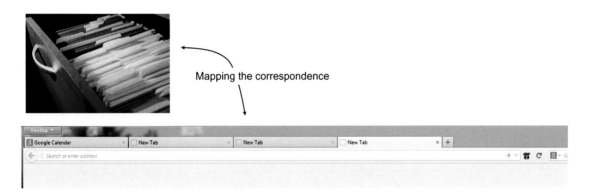

Mapping the correspondence

FIGURE 18.2:
Tabs, as physical places for conceptual elements, have a distinct visual metaphor.

conceptual elements implies some sort of a visual appearance. Tabs are a metaphor to the tabs on files we are familiar with from the real world (Figure 18.2). Does using tabs imply we are going with a desktop-type metaphor? Not necessarily, because it is common to use tabs as places for mutually exclusive conceptual elements, and they have different appearances depending on the interaction channel and its native style. However, we ought to be aware that a metaphor can be "broken" easily. Back to the book metaphor example discussed above, the right-hand picture in Figure 18.1 shows the use of the book metaphor overlaid with a typical toolbar with various functions, which breaks the metaphor and takes the user back to the standard look of computer applications.

Steps to choosing a metaphor:

1. Determine if it is relevant to have a metaphor. Base yourself on outcomes of the user research.
2. Get familiar with users' language and if metaphors are commonly used in their lives, work, society, and culture.
3. Utilize user research to consider mental models.
4. Determine how far you can go with the metaphor (see above the book metaphor as an example for the breakdown of the metaphor).
5. Consider native and conventional metaphors (e.g., file).
6. Consider the product brand.

ADD DETAILS

So far, the conceptual model is at a relatively high abstraction level. Choosing a metaphor can help the transition to adding more details to the conceptual model. Even when assigning the conceptual elements to physical places, the representation was in terms of placeholders with no details in any of the places. However, once we have evaluated and validated the model, it is time to start adding the details. Specifically, add the details from the functional chunks.

The details of each functional chunk are derived from the user research and the analyses that were performed. The details can include the following:

- *Actions*—Distinguish between navigation actions and actions performed on the subject-matter objects. Navigation actions are those that enable going through the navigation map of the conceptual model, for example, opening or closing a window, clicking on a tab to move to another conceptual element, and opening a file or an application. The actions on subject-matter objects can be derived primarily from the object-action analysis. Actions on subject-matter objects can include the creation, modification, or deletion of objects (e.g., creating a new workout plan in the running experience example).
- *Parameters*—Typically, each subject-matter object is associated with parameters that help the user define it. In the running experience example, the planned distance in kilometers is one of the parameters that help the user define the workout. Note that since this step is the transition to the detailed design, but not the fine-tuning and the finalization of the detailed design, there is no need to determine the final user interface element that will let the user define the parameter. For example, the planned distance in kilometers can be set in a

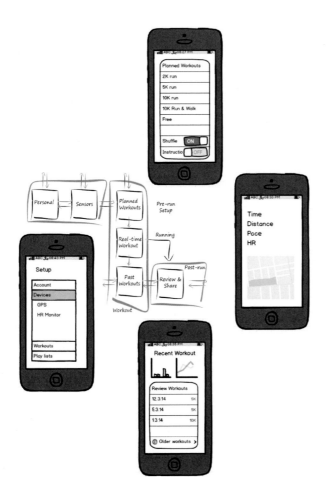

FIGURE 18.3:
Examples of adding details to the prototyped conceptual model in the running experience example (along with the conceptual model in the center).

simple text field, or a text field with a spinner control, or selected from a preset list of distances. The decision on any of these does not need to be completed at this step.

- *Information*—Any information, static or dynamic, that is not user-defined. The information can include any information received from external sources and not entered or set by the user, marketing information, explanations and descriptions, titles and captions, parameter labels, and user guidance (Figure 18.3).

DEVELOP A FULL STORYBOARD

Having added details to the design, and having prototyped it, we can now put everything together into a storyboard. Storyboarding originated in the visual arts,

The first time Jake used the application, he started with the Setup screen. He first set his account and then went on to configure the HR monitor to work with the application while he runs. As part of his planning he went on to define several planned workouts.

From the Setup screen he navigated to the Planned Workouts screen. He setup several workouts according to varying distances he was planning to run at different times.

When he ran, he would glance at the screen of his smart phone, and could see some interesting parameters of his running performance, in addition to a map showing where he was.

Once he completed his run, the application switched to a screen summarizing his most recent run where could view numeric parameters and graphs summarizing his performance. He could also access summaries of previous runs.

FIGURE 18.4:

A partial storyboard for the running experience example with the mobile channel presented as a story.

primarily cinema and video, and later digital media. The fundamental idea is to present in a visual graphic fashion a sequence of episodes in a story. It is used to design and illustrate the sequence in the story. Storyboarding was adapted in the area of requirements gathering (Andriole, 1992), scenario-based design (Carroll, 2000), and user interface design (Landay & Myers, 2001).

The idea of the storyboard as part of the conceptual design process is to represent the full conceptual model in terms of the key interaction flows, according to the scenarios and analyses we have from the user research. The detailed storyboard is a powerful tool for communicating and testing the conceptual model. We can present it as the form of the user scenario (see Figure 18.4).

Another way to present the storyboard is create a navigation map with the key prototyped and detailed conceptual elements in contrast to the navigation map we used so far with boxes-and-arrows representations (Figure 18.5).

TEST AND REVISE

So far, we used inspection tools such as the checklist proposed in the earlier steps for evaluations. We did not have the possibility to collect "real" performance and experience measures. Now, you have a prototyped and detailed conceptual design, and you can run empirical formative testing involving users and usage scenarios, and stakeholders can collect various usability and experience metrics. With the details and the prototype, we have now gained a significant additional capability of evaluation and testing in comparison with the earlier inspections.

Many of the available books and resources on usability testing and measuring user experience are relevant for the testing at this stage. We will not elaborate further on testing in view of the abundance of resources on usability testing and because this book focuses only on the conceptual design phase in the entire life cycle.

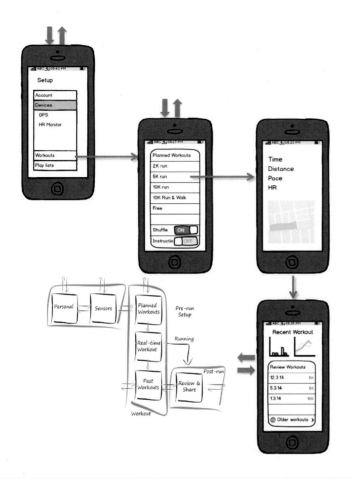

FIGURE 18.5:
A partial storyboard of the running example with the mobile channel presented as a navigation map.

PROJECT MANAGEMENT CONSIDERATIONS

We now have details. Often, the outcome of this design phase is easier to communicate because we can show something concrete, which is easier to understand. We can also test what we have. How can we get to what we see in Figures 18.4 and 18.5 fast, since it feels we went through a long sequence of activities and outcomes that may be harder to communicate and evaluate?

First, as tempting as it is, do not to skip all the steps that led to this point. A good and valid detailed conceptual model must be based on the foundation developed and validated in all previous steps.

Second, remember the teamwork approach. All relevant stakeholders should buy into this process and be an integral part of it.

Third, we discussed earlier how to have the previous steps shorter and faster. Remember, **the goal is not necessarily to follow a linear process but rather ensure that all layers of the design are covered and well integrated at the end.**

Form: Key Practical Points

- Develop the appearance concept and consider using a metaphor.
- Based on the functional chunks, add details to the model.
- Construct a detailed storyboard with a detailed prototype.
- The outcome is a detailed prototype demonstrating the entire conceptual model.
- Test with users, team members, and other stakeholders to validate the model and the interaction.

Summary: Conceptual Design Methodology in a Glance

As a way of summarizing, let us now take the entire methodology and sum it up as a 1-2-3 step process. Here is the idea:

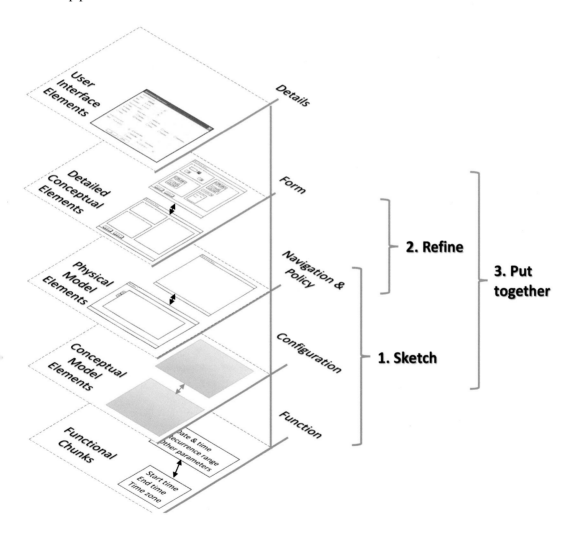

1. *Sketch the conceptual model*: Sketching the conceptual model spans three layers in the framework, from defining functional chunks, to configuring the model, to delineating the navigation map.
2. *Refine it*: Refine the model by assigning elements to physical places, defining the policy, and fine-tuning the navigation and operational principles.
3. *Put everything together*: Finally, put everything together by developing a fully prototyped detailed model.

Along the line of the 1-2-3 process, here is the entire methodology in a single page you can take away with you and use as a quick reference card (Table 19.1):

TABLE 19.1:
Conceptual design methodology map

	1. Sketch	2. Refine	3. Put together
User research	User profiles, Personas, Context, Scenarios, Tasks and workflow, Objects, Business objectives, Usability goals	User profiles, Personas, Context, Tasks and workflow, Objects, Business objectives, Scenarios, Usability goals	User profiles, Personas, Context, Tasks and workflow, Objects, Business objectives, Scenarios, Usability goals
Activities	Define chunks, Define conceptual elements, Configure, Define navigation, Evaluate & Revise	Assign physical places, Define policy, Define Operational Principles, Evaluate & Revise	Metaphor/Appearance concept, Storyboard, Prototype, Test & Revise
Deliverable			
Project	Core team, Stake-holders, Data collection, Schedule, budget, Design reviews	Core team, Stake-holders, Schedule, budget, Design reviews	Core team, Stake-holders, Design reviews, Schedule, budget, Testing participants, Testing facilities
Science	Mental models – the theoretical aspects, Memory and understanding of chunks, Multitasking, workload, stress	Visual search, Familiarity and experience, Motor control fundamentals	Color perception, Testing and evaluation principles, Usability test report

Beyond the conceptual model and onto detailed design

The transition from conceptual to detailed design is part of the same continuous process. Following that, we carry-over into the detailed design goals and issues that we addressed in the conceptual design. Throughout the book we used the following human performance goals as a guide for conceptual design decisions:

- Mental models and understanding
- Location awareness
- Visual search effectiveness
- Operational (executing actions) load
- Working memory load

As we transition into the detailed design, we should continue with these goals in mind. In the same manner each of these goals was translated into conceptual design requirements, now they should be further translated into detailed design requirements. The following table (Table 1) offers some principles and requirements as you move on from conceptual to detailed design:

Human performance goals	Conceptual design	Detailed design
Facilitate intuitive understanding	Express affinities between elements	Layout to convey structure and relations; consistent use of metaphor
Support location awareness	Keep elements in fewer places; Shorten navigation routes required to complete tasks	Navigation controls; titles and captions as clear landmarks
Minimize working memory load		Titles and captions; feedback and information; aids and guides
Reduce operational load		Short-cuts and alternate ways to perform tasks; provide immediate access to operations
Increase visual search effectiveness	Minimize number of functional elements in a single functional chunk	Layout to guide visual search

TABLE 1:
Detailed design guidelines and requirements carried over from conceptual design guidelines to meet human performance goals

References

Andriole, S. J. (1992). *Rapid application prototyping: The storyboard approach to user requirements analysis.* Wellesley, MA: QED Information Sciences, Inc.

Annett, J. (2004). Hierarchical task analysis. In D. Diaper, & N. A. Stanton (Eds.), *The handbook of task analysis for human-computer interaction* (pp. 67–82). Mahwah, NJ: Lawrence Erlbaum.

Brinck, T., Gergle, D., & Wood, S. D. (2002). *Usability for the Web.* San Francisco, CA: Morgan Kaufman Publishers.

Carroll, J. M. (2000). Five reasons for scenario-based design. *Interacting with Computers, 13*(1), 43–60.

Catrambone, R., & Holyoak, K. J. (1989). Overcoming contextual limitations on problem-solving transfer. *Journal of Experimental Psychology: Learning, Memory, and Cognition, 15*(6), 1147.

Diaper, D., & Stanton, N. A. (Eds.). (2004). *The handbook of task analysis for human-computer interaction.* Mahwah, NJ: Lawrence Erlbaum.

Garrett, J. J. (2002). *The elements of user experience: User-centered design for the web and beyond.* London: Pearson Education.

Gick, M. L., & Holyoak, K. J. (1980). Analogical problem solving. *Cognitive Psychology, 12*(3), 306–355.

Gick, M. L., & Holyoak, K. J. (1983). Schema induction and analogical transfer. *Cognitive Psychology, 15*(1), 1–38.

Gothelf, J., & Seiden, J. (2013). *Lean UX: Applying lean principles to improve user experience.* Sebastopol, CA: O'Reilly.

Hackos, J. T., & Redish, J. C. (1998). *User and task analysis for interface design.* New York: Wiley.

Hollnagel, E. (1988). Mental models and model mentality. In L. P. Goodstein, H. B. Andersen, & S. E. Olsen (Eds.), *Task, errors and mental models* (pp. 261–268). Risø National Laboratory, Denmark: Taylor & Francis.

Holyoak, K. J., & Thagard, P. (1995). *Mental leaps: Analogy in creative thought.* Cambridge, MA: MIT Press.

Kirwan, B., & Ainsworth, L. K. (Eds.). (1992). *A guide to task analysis.* London: Taylor & Francis.

Lakoff, G., & Johnson, M. (2003). *Metaphors we live by. 1980.* Chicago, IL: University of Chicago Press.

Landay, J. A., & Myers, B. A. (2001). Sketching interfaces: Toward more human interface design. *Computer, 34*(3), 56–64.

Lewis, D. (1986). *On the plurality of worlds.* Oxford: Basil Blackwell.

Lynch, P. J., & Horton, S. (2008). *Web style guide: Basic design principles for creating Web sites.* New Haven, CT: Yale University Press.

Moray, N. (1987). Intelligent aids, mental models and the theory of machines. *International Journal of Man-Machine Studies, 27*, 619–629.

Mulder, S., & Yaar, Z. (2007). *The user is always right: A practical guide to creating and using personas for the web.* Berkeley, CA: New Riders.

Navon, D. (1977). Forest before trees: The precedence of global features in visual perception. *Cognitive Psychology, 9*, 353–383.

Norman, D. A. (1983). Some observation on mental models. In D. Gentner, & A. Stevens (Eds.), *Mental models* (pp. 7–14). Hillsdale, NJ: Lawrence Erlbaum.

Norman, D. A. (1988). *The design of everyday things.* New York: Doubleday/Currency.

Norman, D. A. (1999). Affordance, conventions, and design. *Interactions, 6*(3), 38–43.

Norman, D. A. (2004). *Emotional design: Why we love (or hate) everyday things.* New York: Basic Books.

Pruitt, J., & Adlin, T. (2006). *The persona lifecycle: Keeping people in mind throughout product design.* San Francisco, CA: Morgan Kaufmann.

Ratcliffe, L., & McNeill, M. (2012). *Agile experience design: A digital designer's guide to agile, lean, and continuous.* Thousand Oaks, CA: New Riders.

Rosson, M. B., & Carroll, J. M. (2002). *Usability engineering: Scenario-based development of human-computer interaction.* San Francisco, CA: Morgan Kaufmann.

Rosson, M. B., & Carroll, J. M. (2009). *Scenario based design. Human-computer interaction.* Boca Raton, FL: CRC Press, pp. 145–162.

Shepherd, A. (2000). HTA as a framework for task analysis. In J. Annett, & N. A. Stanton (Eds.), *Task analysis* (pp. 9–24). London: Taylor & Francis.

Shneiderman, B. (1982). The future of interactive systems and the emergence of direct manipulation. *Behaviour & Information Technology, 1*(3), 237–256.

Shneiderman, B. (1983). Direct manipulation. A step beyond programming languages. *IEEE Computer, 1*(8), 57–69.

Shneiderman, B. (1998). *Designing the user interface.* Reading, MA: Addison-Wesley.

Shneiderman, B., Plaisant, C. (2010). *Designing the user interface: Strategies for effective human-computer interaction* (5th ed., 606 pages). Reading, MA: Addison-Wesley Publ. Co.

Young, R. M. (1981). The machine inside the machine: Users' models of pocket calculators. *International Journal of Man-Machine Studies, 15*, 51–85.

Index

Note: Page numbers followed by *f* indicate figures and *t* indicate tables.

A

Architectural plan, 9, 10*f*
  abstract representation, 9–10
  places, 9
  routes, 9

B

Business context
  business opportunities, 72–73
  generating and increasing revenue, 72
  new technology, 72
  nonrevenue motivations, 72
  user and usage aspects, 71
  user needs, 72

C

Complex conceptual models
  characteristics, 63–64, 64*f*
  flexibility and control, 63–64
  tasks and workflows, 63–64
  unstructured task support, 64, 65
Conceptual design methodology, 11, 12*f*, 137–138
  layered framework, 77, 78*f*
  project management considerations, 78
Conceptual model elements, 41
  architecture plan, 9
  configuration layer
    appointment setup applications, 21, 22*f*
    calendar applications, 21, 23*t*
    connections between, 20–22, 21*f*
    fundamental characteristics, 20
  form layer, 19–20
    fine-tuning, 20
    granularity levels, 20, 21*f*
    metaphor, 20
    navigation policy, 20
  human performance, 43, 46–48, 48*f*
  on location awareness, 44–45
  on mental models, 44

navigation map, 25–27
  considerations, 26
  physical places, 27–29, 27*f*, 28*f*
  route characteristics, 26–27
on operational load, 45
pivotal element, 100–103
project management considerations, 104–105
reconfiguration, 103
revisit and revise, 104
typology of, 51
usability and user experience, 43, 48–50
on visual search, 45
on working memory, 46
Conceptual navigation map, 25–27. *See also* Navigation map
Configuration layer
  conceptual model elements
    appointment setup applications, 21, 22*f*
    calendar applications, 21, 23*t*
    connections between, 20–22, 21*f*
    fundamental characteristics, 20
  functional architecture, 19
Content-oriented chunks, 15, 15*f*
Cross-channel application. *See* Setting an appointment, calendar
    applications

D

Design and development context
  deployment, 75
  design activities, 74
  implementation, 75
  initiation phase, 74
  project management
    multi and cross-channel interaction, 76
    teamwork approach, 76
    user and usage research, 75–76
  research activities, 74
  strategic and business considerations, 75
  testing, 75
  user-oriented approach, 73

Detailed conceptual design, 37–39
    actions, 132
    information, 133
    metaphor, 130–132
    parameters, 132
    project management considerations, 135–136
    storyboard, 133–134
    test and revise, 134

F

Form layer
    conceptual model elements, 37–39
    functional chunks, 132–133
        actions, 132
        information, 133
        parameters, 132
    user interface elements, 39
Functional chunks, 13, 41
    a-priori considerations, 90
    vs. compound chunk, 15–17, 16*f*
    configuration layer, 19–22
    emergent process, 90
    object-oriented, 14, 14*f*, 92, 92*f*, 93*f*, 94–95
    project management considerations, 97–98
    revisit and revise, 97
    task-oriented, 14, 14*f*, 90–92, 91*f*, 93–94

G

Global precedence, 9–10
Granularity levels, 37–38
Graphical user interface (GUI), 3–4

H

Hierarchical conceptual model, 54*f*, 55, 55*f*
    appropriate for, 54
    configuration, 53
    exceptions and variations, 54
    interaction policy, 54
    navigation map, 53
    performance implications, 54
    usability implications, 54
Hierarchical task analysis (HTA), 83–84, 84*f*
Hub and spokes conceptual model, 57, 57*f*, 102–103
    appropriate for, 56
    configuration, 55
    exceptions and variations, 56
    interaction policy, 56

    navigation map, 55–56
    performance implications, 56–57
    usability implications, 56
Human performance implications, 10, 29, 43, 46–48,
        141, 141*t*
    appointment applications, 46
        impacts, 46
        trade-offs, 47
    on location awareness, 44–45
    on mental models, 44
    navigation map, 110, 111*t*
    navigation policy, 114, 115*t*
    on operational load, 45–46
    usability and user experience, 48–50
    on visual search, 45
    on working memory, 46
Hybrid conceptual models, 51, 63

I

Interaction channels, 3

J

Journey and experience map, 86, 87*f*

L

Layered framework, 11, 12*f*
    conceptual design, 77
    conceptual to detailed design, 77
    configuration level, 11
    detailed design, 77
    details level, 11
    form level, 11
    function level, 11
    navigation and policy level, 11
Link functional chunks, 93–97

M

Matrix conceptual model, 58*f*, 59–60, 60*f*
    appropriate for, 59–60
    configuration, 58
    interaction policy, 59
    navigation principles, 58–59
    performance implications, 59
    usability implications, 59
Mental models, 73, 100–101
    elements and links, 43–44
    human performance parameters, 44

metaphor, 39, 130

Norman's definition, 44

object-oriented functional chunks, 92

physical place assignment, 114

potential impacts, 46

task-oriented functional chunks, 90

user and usage research, 79

Metaphor, 130–132

Minimum viable product (MVP), 97–98

Modality, navigation policy, 29, 30

Most viable experience (MVX), 97–98

Multi-channel application. *See* Setting an appointment, calendar applications

Multiple-sequence conceptual model. *See* Hierarchical conceptual model

N

Navigation, 25

Navigation map, 25, 41

appointment setup, 35, 35*t*

conceptual model elements, 25–27

considerations, 26

physical places, 27–29, 27*f*, 28*f*

route characteristics, 26–27

entry and exit conceptual elements, 108

evaluation scenario

conceptual model, 110, 111*t*

human performance, 110, 111*t*

usability and user experience, 110, 111*t*

mobile and desktop channels, 108*f*, 109, 109*f*

model configuration, 26

operational principles, 33–35, 34*t*

project management considerations, 111–112

Navigation policy, 41

appointment setup, 35

channel's operational principles, 122–124, 123*t*

checkpoint, 122

definition, 121, 122*t*

inspection-style evaluation, 124–126, 125*t*

modality, 29

physical place assignment

analyses outcomes and implications, 115–116, 116*t*

business and brand considerations, 117

human performance goals, 114, 115*t*

interaction channel characteristics, 117

prototyping, 118–120, 119*f*

usage context, 116–117

project management considerations, 126–127, 126*t*

Network conceptual model, 61*f*, 62–63, 62*f*

appropriate for, 61

configuration, 60

interaction policy, 61

navigation principles, 60

performance implications, 61

usability implications, 61

Nonsequential and unstructured conceptual models, 51

hub and spokes, 55–57, 56*f*

matrix, 58–60, 58*f*

network, 60–63, 61*f*

O

Object-action analysis, 84–85, 86*t*

abstract objects, 85

people, 84

physical and tangible entities, 85

Object-oriented functional chunks, 14, 14*f*

appropriateness, 92

definition, 92

links, 94–95

P

Pivotal elements, 100–103

Product functionality, 13

Project management considerations

conceptual design methodology, 78

conceptual model elements, 104–105

design and development context

multi and cross-channel interaction, 76

teamwork approach, 76

user and usage research, 75–76

detailed conceptual design, 135–136

functional chunks, 97–98

navigation map, 111–112

navigation policy, 126–127, 126*t*

S

Sequential and structured conceptual models, 51

hierarchical structure, 53–55, 54*f*

single-sequence structure, 52–53, 52*f*

Setting an appointment

calendar applications

smartphone-based interface, 6–7, 6*f*

tablet-based application, 4–6, 5*f*

Setting an appointment *(Continued)*

    Web-based application, 4, 5*f*

      Windows-based GUI application, 3–4, 5*f*

  configuration layer, 21, 22*f*

  functional chunks, 16–17, 17*f*

  human performance implications, 46–48, 48*f*

  navigation map, 35, 35*t*

  navigation policy, 35

  usability implications, 49–50, 49*t*

Single-sequence conceptual model, 52*f*, 53, 53*f*

  appropriate for, 52–53

  configuration, 52

  exceptions and variations, 52

  navigation map, 52

  navigation policy, 52

  performance implications, 52

  usability implications, 52

Smartphone-based interface, appointment setup, 6–7, 6*f*

  date and time, 6

  recurrence, 7

  reminder, 7

  subject and location, 6

Storyboarding, 133–134

T

Tablet-based application, appointment setup, 4–6, 5*f*

  date and time, 4

  purpose and location, 4

  recurrence, 6

  reminder, 6

Task-oriented functional chunks, 14, 14*f*

  appropriateness, 90

  definition, 90

  links, 93–94

U

Usability and user experience, 48–50

  calendar applications, 49–50, 49*t*

  hub and spokes model, 56

  matrix conceptual model, 59

  multiple-sequence model, 53–55

  navigation map, 110, 111*t*

  navigation policy, 124–126, 125*t*

  network conceptual model, 61

  single-sequence model, 52

  usability requirements, 86–87

User and usage research

  business context, 71

  data sources and collection techniques, 79–80, 80*t*

  data types, 80–81, 80*t*

  journey and experience map, 86, 87*f*

  object-action analysis, 84–85, 86*t*

  persona and scenario implications, 82, 83*f*

  scenarios, 81

  strategic aspects, 87–88

  task and workflow analysis, 82–84, 84*f*

  usability requirements, 86–87

  user profiles and personas, 81, 82*f*

User goals, 3

W

Web-based application, appointment setup, 4, 5*f*

  parameters, 4

  recurrence, 4

  reminder, 4

Windows-based GUI application, appointment setup, 3–4, 4*f*, 5*f*

  parameters, 3

  recurrence, 4

  reminder, 3